NO SIGN OF THE ESCAPED ROBOT WE'RE LOOKIN' FOR. I THOUGHT YOU SAID HE WAS HIDING OUT HERE, CUTIE!
AFFIRMATIVE, SAM. ELECTRO-ACTIVITY READINGS INDICATE CLOSE PROXIMITY OF A FUNCTIONING ROBOT. IMPULSE LEVELS CHECK WITH ROBOT FK-2B.

"CUTIE-THAT'S MY ROBOMETER-HAS GOT THE VOICE OF A DUMB BLONDE. BUT SHE'S ALWAYS RIGHT. NEXT SECOND THE ARMCHAIR WAS COMING AT ME LIKE AN EXPRESS CAPSULE.
UUUH!

STAND ASIDE, ROBOHUNTER!
FK2B FRANK
AAAGH! A ROBOT CHAIR!

THESE FURNITURE-SHAPED ROBOTS MAY SAVE SPACE IN THE HOME, BUT THEY SURE MAKE LIFE HELL FOR A ROBOHUNTER-
GOTTA STOP IT. A LIMPET-

"THE LIMPET SENDS A 1000 VOLT CHARGE STRAIGHT TO THE NEURAL BANKS. IT'S THE NEAREST THING TO PAIN A ROBOT WILL EVER KNOW.
FK2B FRANK
ZZz
D1202426

NO... NO MORE ...MASTER. FRANK WILL... OBEY!
YOU BETTER BELIEVE IT, FRANK. AND JUST TO MAKE SURE I'M GONNA DO A LITTLE WORK ON YOUR CIRCUITS!

"I REPAIRED FRANK'S OBEDIENCE BANKS, THEN ADJUSTED MY BLASTER TO A BLOW-TORCH FLAME. THE GOVERNMENT PAYS A BOUNTY ON EVERY ESCAPED ROBOT-"
JUST CUT OFF THE SERIAL NUMBERS AN' HAND 'EM IN AT ROBOT CONTROL. AIN'T MUCH, BUT IT ALL HELPS TO PAY THE RENT.
"I RODE FRANK ACROSS CITY TO MY OFFICE. BY RIGHTS NO ROBOT SHOULD GO WRONG. THEY WERE PROGRAMMED NEVER TO GO WRONG. BUT THEY ALWAYS DID."
"I SHOULD KNOW. I'VE MADE MY LIVING CATCHING THEM FOR FORTY YEARS."

"FORTY YEARS... A LONG TIME. SOONER OR LATER ONE OF THOSE METAL MONSTERS IS GOING TO CRUNCH ME UP. THAT'S HOW IT ALWAYS ENDS FOR A ROBOHUNTER."

"WHEN I GOT TO MY OFFICE, CARLTON, THE B.S.C. (BUILDING SURVEILLANCE COMPUTER) HAD A MESSAGE -"
HEY, SLADE! THERE'S SOME DAME WAITING FOR YOU IN YOUR OFFICE. A REAL GOOD LOOKER, SHE IS. SAID HER NAME WAS WINTERS!
WINTERS-THAT'S YOUR OWNER, FRANK. COME ON!

ROBO-HUNTER
VERDUS

ROBO-HUNTER CREATED BY

JOHN WAGNER AND IAN GIBSON

VERDUS

Script: John Wagner

Art: Ian Gibson, José Luis Ferrer

Letters: Steve Potter, Thom, Pete Knight

Originally published in *2000 AD* Progs 76-82 and 100-112

ROBO-HUNTER

"I CAME INTO THE APARTMENT BLASTING. I'VE BEEN AT THIS GAME FOR FORTY YEARS AND THERE'S ONE THING I'VE LEARNED- NEVER GIVE A ROBOT AN EVEN BREAK-"

THE NAME'S SLADE, SAM SLADE! THAT'S S-L-A-Y-E-D TO YOU!

2000 A.D.
Credit Card:

SCRIPT ROBOT
T. B. GROVER

ART ROBOT
FERRER/GIBSON

LETTERING ROBOT
PETE KNIGHT

COMPU·73E

GIBSON

"HA HA, JUST MY LITTLE JOKE. BUT THESE ROBOTS WEREN'T LAUGHING."
"WHEN THEY GET SLADE, THEY STAY SLADE - THAT'S MY MOTTO."
BZZZZZP.
K-RR-RZZZZTT!
"THE BIG ROBOT WITH THE TWO-TON MITTS WASN'T LAUGHING EITHER-"
DESTROY! DESTROY!
UHHH! SHOULDA... SEEN HIM COMIN'... YOU'RE GETTIN'-OLD-SAM-
DESTREEEEEEEEE!
BUT NOT SO OLD I'M FIXIN' TO CROAK JUST YET. A QUICK ELBOW TO THE CIRCUIT HATCH-
K-RR-RZZZTT!
"THAT JANGLED HIS CIRCUITS LONG ENOUGH FOR ME TO SEND HIM TO THAT GREAT SCRAP HEAP IN THE SKY!"

"I CHECKED HER OUT BEFORE I WENT IN. THE OLD SAM SLADE SNIFFER WAS GIVING ME THOSE DANGER SIGNALS AGAIN..."
SHE CAN'T KNOW I'VE CAUGHT HER ROBOT, SO WHAT'S SHE DOIN' HERE..?

OH, MR SLADE! YOU-YOU'VE CAUGHT MY FRANK! WHAT CAN I EVER DO TO REPAY YOU?
CAREFUL, HONEY. I MIGHT TELL YOU!
CLUB

OH, MR SLADE... COULD YOU REALLY FALL FOR A SILLY LITTLE THING LIKE ME..?
"SHE WAS A GOOD LOOKER ALL RIGHT. TOO GOOD. AND SOMETHING TOLD ME THAT SPARKLE IN HER EYE WASN'T LOVE'S FLAME."

"MY FIRST PUNCH DROVE INTO HER CHIN LIKE A PILEDRIVER."
SORRY, BABY, BUT I'VE NEVER SEEN A REAL, LIVE WOMAN WHO WAS PERFECT. WHICH YOU ARE!
KROK!

"ONE PUNCH WAS ENOUGH. HER HEAD HIT THE WALL WITH A METAL THUD..."
LIKE I THOUGHT-A ROBOT. AN' A ROBOT THAT POSES AS HUMAN IS UP TO NO GOOD!

"HIT FIRST AND ASK QUESTIONS LATER, THAT'S WHAT I ALWAYS SAY. UNFORTUNATELY THIS ROBOT WASN'T GOING TO DO ANY MORE TALKING."
DOGGONE IT, CUTIE! WHY DIDN'T YOU WARN ME ABOUT HER?
DON'T BLAME YOUR ROBOMETER, SLADE. THE MRS WINTERS ROBOT WAS SHIELDED AGAINST DETECTION!

"AS I TURNED ROUND I FOUND TWO GOOKS IN THE DOORWAY... MY DOORWAY."
ROGERS AND CHAN. INTERNATIONAL SPACE COMMISSION. THE MRS WINTERS ROBOT WAS OURS, AND YOU'VE JUST PASSED THE TEST!
HEY, WHAT IS THIS? LISTEN, YOU MONKEYS, NOBODY PLAYS GAMES WITH SAM SLADE!

THIS IS BUSINESS, SLADE. WE'VE GOT A JOB FOR THE BEST ROBO-TECTIVE IN THE BUSINESS, AND YOU JUST PROVED THAT YOU'RE IT!
PAY VERY CLOSE ATTENTION, MR SLADE!

"CHARLIE CHAN PLUGGED AN INFORMATION SLUG INTO MY VIDEO AND THEN THEY LAID IT ON ME-"
DATELINE 2080, SLADE-THAT'S SIXTY YEARS AGO. THE OVERPOPULATION OF THE EARTH HAD REACHED SUCH CRISIS PROPORTIONS THAT THE INTERNATIONAL SPACE COMMISSION SENT OUT AN UNMANNED FASTER-THAN-LIGHT SPACECRAFT TO SEARCH FOR A NEW WORLD!
FOUR YEARS LATER IT FOUND ONE-VERDUS-IN THE CRAB NEBULA. A PLANET PERFECT IN EVERY RESPECT FOR HUMAN LIFE-A REAL PROMISED LAND!

"AT THE TIME IT WAS STILL IMPOSSIBLE TO SEND HUMANS AT SPEEDS FASTER THAN LIGHT. INSTEAD WE SENT A ROBOT-SJ1, A PRIMITIVE MODEL CONVERTED TO BURN SOLID FUEL..."
"GOOD LUCK SMOKIN' JOE"
"SJ1'S MISSION WAS TO BUILD OTHER ROBOTS-AND TOGETHER TO FASHION A WORLD FIT TO RECEIVE HUMANS..."

"SIX YEARS LATER THE SIGNAL CAME BACK-ROBOTS WERE AT WORK. VERDUS WAS READY..."
"BUT IT WASN'T UNTIL 2110-ONLY THIRTY YEARS AGO-THAT THE PROBLEMS OF FASTER-THAN-LIGHT TRAVEL WERE FINALLY SOLVED AND THE FIRST COLONISTS WERE SENT OUT..."
"WE'RE GOING TO THE PROMISED LAND"
VERDUS OR BUST
HAPPY DAYS

WE KNOW THE COLONISTS ARRIVED ON VERDUS, MR SLADE. BUT THAT IS ALL. THEY WERE NEVER HEARD FROM AGAIN.
FURTHER PARTIES WERE SENT OUT, INCLUDING CRACK SPACE TROOPS. ALL SIGNALLED THEIR ARRIVAL ON VERDUS-AND THEN NOTHING. THEY JUST DISAPPEARED WITHOUT TRACE!
A SWELL LITTLE MYSTERY. BUT WHERE DO I COME IN?

WE BELIEVE THE ROBOTS HAVE GONE WRONG AND TAKEN OVER. IT IS A PROBLEM THAT REQUIRES THE BEST ROBOT MAN IN THE BUSINESS. THAT MAN IS YOU, SLADE.
YOU'RE CRAZY! IF ROBOTS HAVE TAKEN OVER, THE PLANET'S A DEATH TRAP! NO, ROGERS, FIND SOME OTHER SUCKER!

YOU'RE THE ONLY SUCKER WE'VE GOT, SLADE-AND TIME IS RUNNING OUT. YOU'LL GO. YOU'LL GO BECAUSE WE TELL YOU TO!
WE ARE POWERFUL ORGANISATION, MR SLADE. WE GIVE YOU CHOICE. STRONG POSSIBILITY OF DEATH ON VERDUS...OR CERTAINTY OF BULLET IN HEAD IF YOU REFUSE.

"SOME CHOICE! IF ROBOTS HAD TAKEN OVER VERDUS I'D HAVE ONE CHANCE IN A THOUSAND OF COMING OUT ALIVE-WHICH IS ONLY SLIGHTLY BETTER ODDS THAN A BULLET IN THE HEAD..."
OKAY, YOU RATS-YOU GOT YOURSELF A SUCKER!
NOW GET OUTA HERE AND LEAVE ME ALONE. I GOT A FEW THINGS TO DO BEFORE I GO!

"ROGERS AND CHAN LEFT, AND I OPENED THE WINDOW TO LET OUT THE STINK-"
CHEER UP, SAM. YOU AND ME, WE'LL HANDLE THOSE ROBOTS!
SPEAK FOR YOURSELF, CUTIE. ME-I'M WRITING MY WILL.
NEXT PROG: THE ONE-WAY TRIP!

DATELINE: 2084. VERDUS, THE PARADISE PLANET, DISCOVERED IN THE DISTANT CRAB NEBULA. A LUSH HAVEN FOR LIFE, IT IS THE LAST HOPE FOR EARTH'S OVERCROWDED BILLIONS.

DATELINE: 2085. ROBOT SJI SENT TO VERDUS. ITS MISSION: TO BUILD OTHER ROBOTS— AND TOGETHER TO FASHION A WORLD FIT TO RECEIVE HUMANS.

DATELINE: 2110. FIRST COLONISTS SIGNAL ARRIVAL ON VERDUS. THEY ARE NEVER HEARD FROM AGAIN. FURTHER PARTIES ALSO DISAPPEAR WITHOUT TRACE.

DATELINE: 2140. SITUATION DESPERATE. EARTH AUTHORITIES SUSPECT ROBOT MALFUNCTION. THEY TURN FOR HELP TO ONE MAN-CRACK ROBOT DETECTIVE, SAM SLADE.

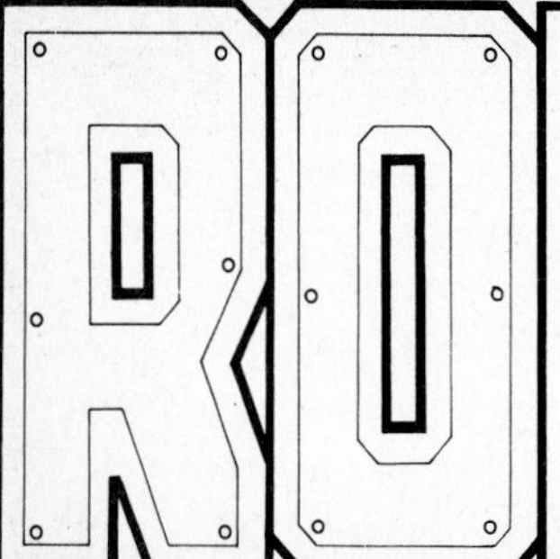

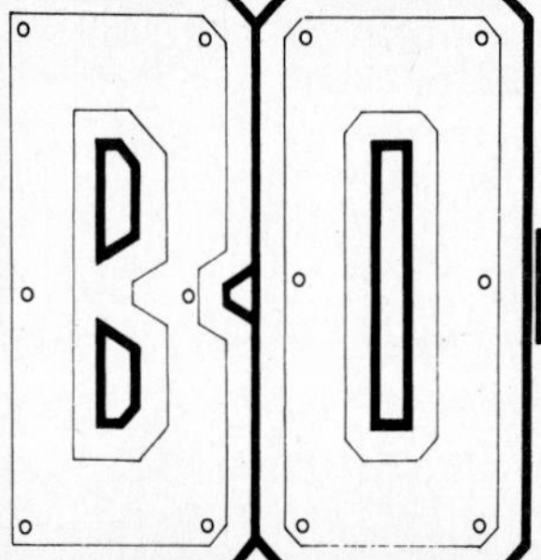

"I LEFT EARTH ON A FRIDAY— FRIDAY THE 13th, TO BE EXACT. I'M NOT ONE FOR SUPERSTITION, BUT I DIDN'T NEED A CALENDAR TO TELL ME THIS **WAS NOT** MY LUCKY DAY."

LIFT-OFF NOW COMPLETE! ANTI-GRAV FUNCTIONING. WARP 9.

K.L.7

"MY STOMACH TOOK AN INSTANT TRIP TO MY SHOES AND THEN SLIPPED BACK INTO PLACE AS WE LEFT THE EARTH'S GRAVITATIONAL PULL."

2000 A.D. Credit Card:

SCRIPT ROBOT MIKE STOTT

ART ROBOT FERRER/GIBSON

LETTERING ROBOT STEVE POTTER

COMPU-73E

"THE NAME'S SLADE, SAM SLADE. OCCUPATION— SUCKER."
ONE DAY I'M A ROBO-HUNTER WORKING MEGACITY. JUST QUIETLY DOIN' MY JOB AND LOOKIN' FORWARD TO COLLECTING MY RETIREMENT PAPERS—
—THE NEXT, I'M ON A FLECTRON DRIVE SHIP HEADING FOR SOME GODFORSAKEN BALL OF MUD THOUSANDS OF LIGHT YEARS AWAY— WITH A BUNCH OF MANIAC ROBOTS WAITIN' FOR ME AT THE OTHER END. SOME FUN!

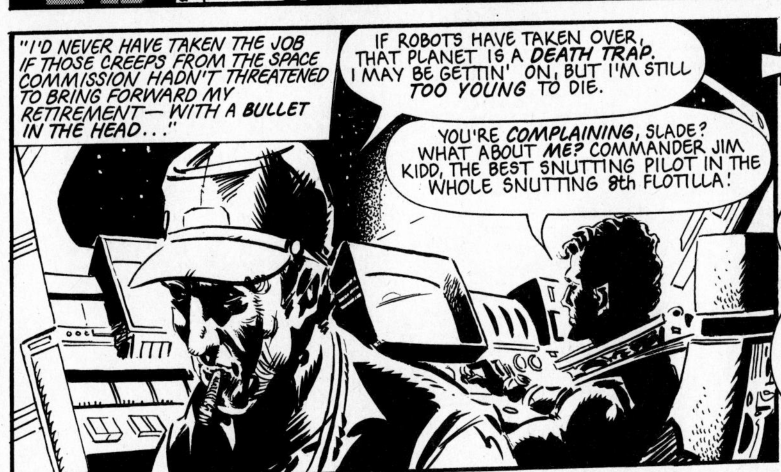
"I'D NEVER HAVE TAKEN THE JOB IF THOSE CREEPS FROM THE SPACE COMMISSION HADN'T THREATENED TO BRING FORWARD MY RETIREMENT— WITH A BULLET IN THE HEAD..."
IF ROBOTS HAVE TAKEN OVER, THAT PLANET IS A DEATH TRAP. I MAY BE GETTIN' ON, BUT I'M STILL TOO YOUNG TO DIE.
YOU'RE COMPLAINING, SLADE? WHAT ABOUT ME? COMMANDER JIM KIDD, THE BEST SNUTTING PILOT IN THE WHOLE SNUTTING 8th FLOTILLA!

"I DON'T KNOW WHAT "SNUTTING" MEANT, BUT I GUESSED IT WASN'T NICE. COMMANDER KIDD WAS THE KIND OF GUY YOU WOULDN'T DREAM OF TAKING HOME TO MOTHER..."
JUST 'COS I SASSED SOME SNUTTING JAP ADMIRAL ON THAT LAST PLUTO RUN THEY SEND ME ON THIS SNUTTING SUICIDE MISSION!
AW, WELL, WHAT THE SNUT! BETTER STRAP IN, SLADE. FLECTRON DRIVE'LL BE SWITCHING ON IN TWO MINUTES.

"IT SEEMED THE ONLY ONE HAPPY WITH THIS JOY RIDE WAS CUTIE, MY ROBOMETER—"
GEE, SAM, THIS IS EXCITING. I'VE NEVER TRAVELLED FASTER THAN LIGHT BEFORE. YOU THINK WE'LL HIT A METEOR SHOWER? A COMET MAYBE?
OH, SNUT UP.

"THE FLECTRON DRIVE CAME ON WITH A HIGH-PITCHED WHINE. THEN THINGS STARTED TO GO HAYWIRE—"
THE SHIELDS— THEY— THEY'RE NOT OPERATING! GOTTA... STOP ... THE FLECTRON DRIVE!

WON'T... WON'T... BUDGE! WE'RE GOING... THROUGH THE LIGHT BARRIER... WITHOUT SAFETY-SHIELDS...!

"THE Gs CAME ON FAST. MY HEAD FELT LIKE AN ORANGE BEING PEELED BY A ROBO-DOZER. IT WAS NOT FUNNY."
AAAAHHH!
YOU OK, SAM? SAM!

"I DON'T KNOW HOW LONG IT LASTED. IT SEEMED LIKE HOURS. THE ONLY THING CERTAIN WAS THE PAIN."
AAAAAHHHHHH!

"THEN, SUDDENLY, THE FLECTRON DRIVE CUT OUT—"
IT—IT'S STOPPED. I'M... I'M STILL ALIVE...
GOSH, SAM! LOOK! LOOK AT YOUR FACE!

IT-IT'S... YOUNGER! JUST LIKE... LIKE I LOOKED WHEN I WAS... 25!

"BEHIND ME THE SCREEN SUDDENLY CLICKED ON. IT WAS ROGERS, THE GOOK WHO'D SUCKERED ME IN ON THIS JOB."
THIS IS A PRERECORDED MESSAGE. BY NOW, SLADE—IF YOU ARE NOT DEAD—YOU WILL HAVE DISCOVERED THE EFFECT OF UNSHIELDED FASTER-THAN-LIGHT TRAVEL ON THE HUMAN BODY. THIS PROCESS IS CAUSED BY...
YOU BLACK-MAILER! CUT THE TECHNICAL GOBBLEDIGOOP AND LAY IT ON ME STRAIGHT.
"BUT YOU CAN NEVER BEAT A TELERECORDING. I DECIDED TO LISTEN."

...SO YOU SEE, SLADE, YOU WERE THE ONLY MAN FOR THE JOB — BUT YOU WERE TOO OLD. WE NEEDED YOU IN YOUR PRIME. WE CALCULATE THE DURATION OF SHIELD MALFUNCTION WILL REVERSE YOUR AGE BY APPROXIMATELY 35 YEARS.

WHAT HAPPENED TO THE PILOT WAS UNFORTUNATE, BUT NECESSARY. HE SHOULD STILL BE OF SOME HELP TO YOU.

I FORGOT ABOUT COMMANDER KIDD! HE WAS A LOT YOUNGER THAN ME—

WAAAAAAAH!

HOLY JOE SMITH! A BABY!

OH, SAM, ISN'T HE A LITTLE DARLING?

COOCHIE COO! YOU'D BETTER STOP CRYING OR UNCLE SAMMY-WAMMY WILL HAVE TO PUT A GAGGY-WAGGY ON YOU...
WAAH!

YOU JUST TRY IT, YOU BIG APE, AN' YOU'LL GET MY BOOTY-WOOTY IN YOUR SNUTTING MOUTHY-WOUTHY! I'M STILL CAPTAIN OF THIS SNUTTING SHIP AND DON'T YOU FORGET IT!
YOU CAN TALK! BUT YOU WERE CRYING LIKE A BABY—

YOU'D BE CRYING TOO IF THIS HAD HAPPENED TO YOU! THOSE SNUTTING RATS! IF I EVER GET OUT OF THIS MESS I'LL PAY THEM BACK IN SPADES! NOW GET ME OUTA THESE RAGS, SLADE.

WHAT'S THAT SMELL? POO— YOU DIRTY DEVIL! YOU'VE DONE NAUGHTIES!
WELL, I CAN'T HELP IT— I'M JUST A SNUTTING BABY, SLADE! SO WHY DONT YOU STOP TURNING UP YOUR NOSE AND GET ME CHANGED?

NOT ON YOUR LIFE, KIDD. I SIGNED ON THIS PLEASURE TRIP AS A ROBO-HUNTER— NOT A NANNY.
ESTIMATED TIME OF THE ARRIVAL
2.1.34
THINK AGAIN, BUSTER. TIME DISTORTION DURING FASTER-THAN-LIGHT TRAVEL MAKES HOURS SEEM LIKE MINUTES. THIS SHIP IS GOING TO ENTER VERDUS ORBIT IN TWO HOURS.
YOU'RE GOING TO NEED ME TO PILOT YOU IN! AND I DON'T GO IN UNLESS I GO IN CLEAN!

"I FOUND WHAT I NEEDED IN STORES. I'M NOT THE MOTHERING TYPE, BUT IT DOESN'T PAY TO ARGUE WITH YOUR PILOT, EVEN IF HE IS ONLY PINT-SIZED..."
DID ANYONE EVER TELL YOU, KIDD— YOU WERE A REAL UGLY BABY.
A LITTLE MORE POWDER THERE, SLADE. WOULDN'T WANT ME GETTING NAPPY RASH, WOULD YOU?

"THE TWO HOURS PASSED QUICKLY. THE SHIP GRADUALLY DECREASED SPEED AS IT APPROACHED THE VERDUS SURFACE—"
LANDING AREA BEARING 090. TWO SECOND BURST ON YOUR PORT RETROS, SLADE. ATTABOY!

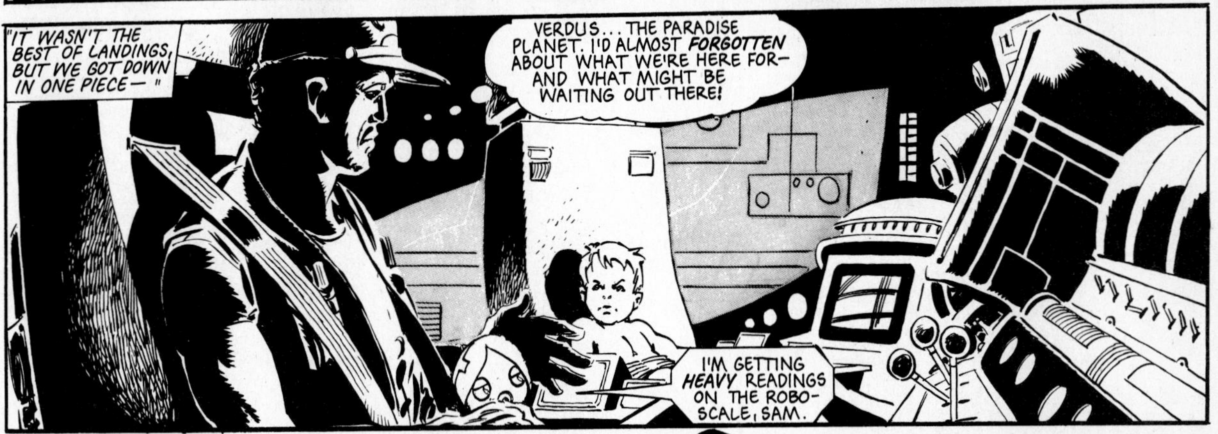
"IT WASN'T THE BEST OF LANDINGS, BUT WE GOT DOWN IN ONE PIECE—"
VERDUS... THE PARADISE PLANET. I'D ALMOST FORGOTTEN ABOUT WHAT WE'RE HERE FOR— AND WHAT MIGHT BE WAITING OUT THERE!
I'M GETTING HEAVY READINGS ON THE ROBO-SCALE, SAM.

"THERE WAS ONE WAY TO FIND OUT. I PRESSED A BUTTON AND THE EXIT PANEL SLID OPEN. I SHOULD HAVE KEPT IT CLOSED—"
WELL, THEY'VE GOT A SNUTTING RECEPTION COMMITTEE, ALL RIGHT—

YEAH, BUT IT DOESN'T LOOK TOO FRIENDLY!
VERDUS: WELCOME TO PARADISE!
NEXT PROG: THE WELCOME

ROBO-HUNTER

"SAM SLADE'S THE NAME, SUICIDE'S THE GAME. AT LEAST, THAT'S THE WAY THINGS WERE SHAPING UP."

"BEING AN ACE ROBOHUNTER, I'D BEEN CHOSEN BY THE **INTERNATIONAL SPACE COMMISSION** TO INVESTIGATE THE STRANGE DISAPPEARANCE OF EARTH SETTLERS ON THE PLANET **VERDUS**. THEY FELT THERE MIGHT BE SOME MAL-FUNCTION IN THE ROBOTS WHO'D BEEN ORDERED TO PREPARE THE PLANET FOR COLONISATION. **THEY WERE RIGHT**—"

"VERDUS WELCOME TO PARADISE"

HOLY JOE SMITH! THAT HEAT SHIELD IS 14 INCHES THICK—AND THEY'RE BURNING THROUGH IT LIKE IT WAS **CANDLE WAX!**

POLICE 5

2000 A.D.
Credit Card:
SCRIPT ROBOT T.B. GROVER
ART ROBOT FERRER/GIBSON
LETTERING ROBOT STEVE POTTER
COMPU·73E

COME ON, SLADE—**YOU'RE** MEANT TO BE THE BIG ROBOT KILLER. **DO SOMETHING!**

"COMMANDER JIM KIDD WAS THE PILOT OF MY FLECTRON DRIVE SHIP—OR HE **HAD BEEN** UNTIL A SHIELD BREAKDOWN HAD TURNED HIM INTO A **ONE-YEAR-OLD**."
"THAT'S A LOT OF NASTINESS TO GET INTO A SMALL PACKAGE—"
GOING TO TRY AND MAKE A **BREAK** FOR IT, KIDD. 'FRAID I'M GOING TO HAVE TO LEAVE YOU BEHIND. CAN'T FIGHT WITH MY HANDS FULL.
THAT'S RIGHT—SAVE YOUR OWN SKIN AND LEAVE ME TO THOSE **METAL FRANKENSTEINS!** YOU SNUTTING **RAT**, SLADE!

"SNUTTING RAT I MAY BE—**BUT THERE ISN'T A BETTER ROBOT MAN IN THE BUSINESS!**"
HEAT SHIELD COMING UP! SEE HOW YOU LIKE THEM APPLES, ROBOHOODS!

SEIZE THE SIM!
WHAT THE HECK–? THAT BLASTER WOULD HAVE BLOWN ANY EARTH ROBOT TO FRAGMENTS!
TRY A LIMPET, SAM.

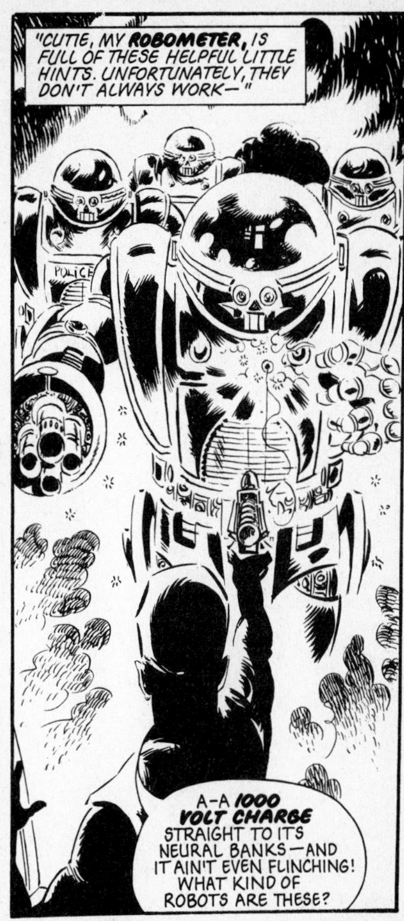
"CUTIE, MY ROBOMETER, IS FULL OF THESE HELPFUL LITTLE HINTS. UNFORTUNATELY, THEY DON'T ALWAYS WORK–"
POLICE
A-A 1000 VOLT CHARGE STRAIGHT TO ITS NEURAL BANKS—AND IT AIN'T EVEN FLINCHING! WHAT KIND OF ROBOTS ARE THESE?

H-HEELP!
GRAB HIM, POLICE 5.
WELCOME TO PARADISE, SIM!

"NEXT SECOND I WAS BEING SHOVED INTO A SET OF JAWS THAT WOULD'VE GIVEN MY DENTIST NIGHTMARES–"
D-DON'T TELL ME THESE THINGS EAT PEOPLE!
GOODBYE, SAM. IT'S BEEN NICE WORKING WITH YOU.

AAAAH!

"MOMENTS LATER, I CAME TO– MY HEAD FELT LIKE IT'D BEEN LEFT UPSTAIRS WITH KIDD."
WE APPEAR TO BE IN A CELL, SAM.
YEAH, A TEN-TON WALKING ALCATRAZ! OH BOY, WELCOME TO DROKKING PARADISE!

"KIDD DROPPED IN A MOMENT LATER. SOMETIMES IT PAYS TO BE A BABY. LIKE, I'M TOO BIG TO CRY — BUT I SURE FELT LIKE IT!"
FORGET ABOUT HIM, CUTIE—CONCENTRATE ON LOOKIN' AFTER ME!
THERE THERE, LITTLE DARLING. DON'T WORRY. CUTIE'S HERE TO LOOK AFTER YOU.
WAAAAAAA!

LISTEN, YOU OVERGROWN SCRAP-HEAP— ROBOTS HAVE GOT TO OBEY HUMANS!
NATURALLY. AN ORDER FROM A HUMAN IS A SACRED COMMAND.
THEN I ORDER YOU TO STOP MESSING ABOUT AND LET US OUTA HERE!

HE ORDERS US TO LET THEM GO! ORDERS US!
HAA HA
HAHA
HA!HAA HAA!.. HA HA HA
HA..HAA..

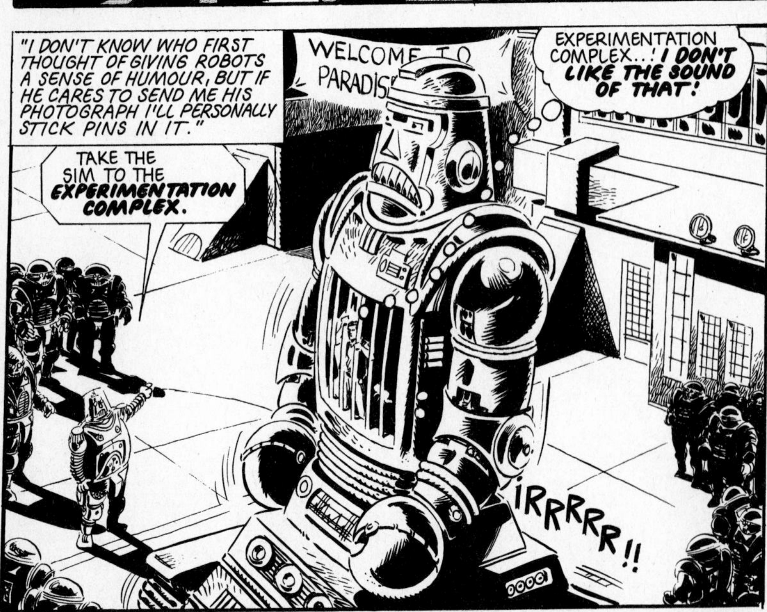
"I DON'T KNOW WHO FIRST THOUGHT OF GIVING ROBOTS A SENSE OF HUMOUR, BUT IF HE CARES TO SEND ME HIS PHOTOGRAPH I'LL PERSONALLY STICK PINS IN IT."
WELCOME TO PARADIS
EXPERIMENTATION COMPLEX...! I DON'T LIKE THE SOUND OF THAT!
TAKE THE SIM TO THE EXPERIMENTATION COMPLEX.
IRRRRR!!

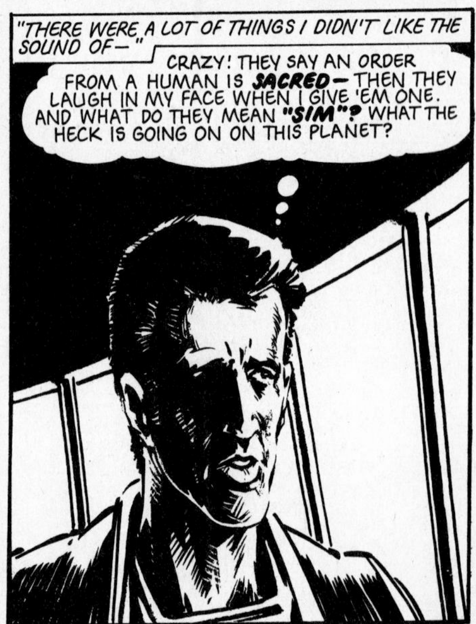
"THERE WERE A LOT OF THINGS I DIDN'T LIKE THE SOUND OF—"
CRAZY! THEY SAY AN ORDER FROM A HUMAN IS SACRED— THEN THEY LAUGH IN MY FACE WHEN I GIVE 'EM ONE. AND WHAT DO THEY MEAN "SIM"? WHAT THE HECK IS GOING ON ON THIS PLANET?

"FLANKED BY POLICE 5 AND POLICE 124, THE PRISON ROBOT CARRIED US THROUGH THE CITY— **AND WHAT A CITY!** IT MADE AN EARTH CITY LOOK LIKE HICKSVILLE—"

JUST LOOK AT IT, SAM! CINEMAS, RESTAURANTS PLEASURE DOMES, MOVING SIDEWALKS, TEN KINDS OF TRANSPORT— THIS PLACE HAS GOT **EVERYTHING!**

YEAH, **EVERYTHING** EXCEPT PEOPLE. WHERE ARE THE **PEOPLE,** CUTIE?

CINE CI

RESTAURANT

POLICE 5

POLICE 124

POLICE 5

THE EXPERIMENTATION COMPLEX WAS HUGE—
EXPERIMENTATION CO
OH, SNUT, LOOK AT THIS PLACE! YOU USELESS HUNK OF ROBOT BAIT, SLADE— **WHAT HAVE YOU GOT US INTO?**
I DUNNO, KIDD— BUT I'LL LAY YOU TEN TO ONE IT **AIN'T** GONNA BE NO HONEYMOON.
YOU MAY PROCEED ALONE, UTILITY 57.
HOLY JOE SMITH! NOW I KNOW WHAT HAPPENED TO THE PEOPLE!

GOSH, SAM! **ROWS AND ROWS OF CAGES!** THEY GO ON FOR **MILES** AND **MILES!**

OH, SNUT— THIS... THIS IS SOME KIND OF **CONCENTRATION CAMP!**

THERE'S A **NEW** ADMISSION! HEY, BUDDY! **I GOT SOMETHING TO TELL YOU!**
WHAT IS IT? TELL ME!

WELCOME TO PARADISE! HA HA HA HA HA HA
JA JA JA.. JA..

WELCOME TO PARADISE
THEY'RE CRAZY, SLADE! THEY'RE ALL **STARK, SNUTTING CRAZY!**
THEN WE BETTER START SAYING OUR **PRAYERS,** KIDD — 'COS WHATEVER HAPPENED TO THEM IS SURE AS SHOOT GONNA HAPPEN TO **US!**
HA HA HA HA HA
NEXT PROG: PARADISE LOST!

ROBO-HUNTER
"ROBOTS HAD TAKEN OVER THE PLANET VERDUS— ROBOTS LIKE I'D NEVER SEEN BEFORE— AND IN THE HUGE "EXPERIMENTATION COMPLEX" I DISCOVERED WHAT HAD HAPPENED TO THE EARTH SETTLERS."
"THEY WERE SETTLED ALL RIGHT. IN CAGES."
"FOR SAM SLADE, ROBO-HUNTER EXTRAORDINAIRE, AND COMMANDER KIDD, PILOT TURNED ONE-YEAR OLD* IT LOOKED LIKE THE END WAS NIGH!"
HAHAHA!
HAHAHA!
WELCOME TO PARADISE!
HAHAHA!
NO WONDER EARTH LOST CONTACT WITH THE SETTLERS! IT'S A CONCENTRATION CAMP!
POOR DEVILS! HALF OUT OF THEIR MINDS!
2000 A.D. Credit Card:
SCRIPT ROBOT T.B. GROVER
ART ROBOT IAN GIBSON
LETTERING ROBOT STEVE POTTER
COMPU·73E
*THARG NOTE: THE EFFECT OF TRAVELLING AT FASTER-THAN-LIGHT SPEEDS WAS TO REDUCE THE AGE OF A HUMAN — AS BOTH SLADE AND KIDD HAD DISCOVERED.

"THEN THE BOTTOM DROPPED OUT OF OUR WORLD—OR AT LEAST THE WALKING ALCATRAZ CALLED UTILITY 57—"
BUT WHY? WHY HAVE THE ROBOTS GONE WRONG? WHY ARE THEY DOING THIS?
AAAH!
WAAH!
YEOW!
OOF!
AAAH!
THAT WILL BE ALL, UTILITY 57. KEEPER 1 WILL TAKE CHARGE OF THE SIMS.*
*THARG NOTE: 'SIMS' WAS THE NAME THE ROBOTS USED FOR HUMANS.

"IT WAS ALL TOO MUCH FOR KIDD. ME, I HAD TO OPEN MY BIG MOUTH—"
WHADDYA MEAN "SIMS"? LISTEN, ROBOT, WE'RE—
AAAGH!
BE SILENT FOR THE EXAMINATION!
WAAAAA!

"IT WAS THE CRAZIEST EXAMINATION I'D EVER HAD. THEY BREED THEIR DOCS NASTY ON VERDUS—"

X-RAY REVEALS NO BIONICS, NO CIRCUITRY. NORMAL BONE SIM INFRA-STRUCTURE SURROUNDED BY TYPICAL SIM ORGANIC MATTER.

AGREED.

AAAH! CUT IT OUT!

REACTION TO PAIN TEST—**SENSITIVE.** WILL NOW TEST FOR **INTELLIGENCE.**

WHAT IS THE **EXPANSION RATIO** OF 1 TO 5 ON THE **MODIFIED ELEMENTAL SCALE?**

ANSWER, SIM.

HUHHH?

AS EXPECTED, TYPICAL **SUB-INTELLIGENT** SIMS. PLACE THEM IN HOLDING PEN 26687, KEEPER 1. THEY WILL BE **RECYCLED** UNDER SCHEDULE F.

THEY MAY KEEP THEIR CLOTHING AND OTHER TOYS, BUT **NOT** THIS PRIMITIVE BLASTER.

HEY, WAIT A MINUTE! WHAT'S ALL THIS **SIM** BUSINESS? I GOT A FEW QUESTIONS TO ASK YOU JOKERS!

SILENCE! SIMS ARE NOT PERMITTED TO QUESTION ROBOTS!
WAAA!
ERK!
"AND THAT, DEAR READERS, WAS THAT."
WELL, AT LEAST THEY LET US HAVE OUR CLOTHES BACK. WHADDYA RECKON THAT ROBOT MEANT BY "RECYCLED UNDER SCHEDULE F", KIDD?
I DON'T KNOW, SLADE! THERE'S A CLIPBOARD UP THERE— HAVE A LOOK AT THAT!
DO NOT FEED! TO BE PROCESSED AS FERTILISER SOONEST!
FERTILISER! WELL, YOU'VE REALLY DROPPED US IN IT NOW, SLADE! AND I THOUGHT YOU WERE SUPPOSED TO BE THE GREAT ROBOHUNTER!
HEY, THAT'S MY LAST CIGAR!
YOU RAT, SLADE! I'VE GOT AS MUCH RIGHT TO A LAST SMOKE AS YOU HAVE!
UH UH! SMOKING IS BAD FOR LITTLE BABIES. GIVE THE STOGIE TO UNCLE SAMMY OR UNCLE SAMMY WILL HAVE TO BELT YOU!
"I SMOKED THE STOGIE AND WATCHED AS PRISONER UPON PRISONER WAS TAKEN AWAY."
ANOTHER SHIPMENT OF HUMAN FODDER— BOUND FOR PARADISE AT THE FERTILISER PLANT, NO DOUBT.
HEY, SAM, LISTEN— I'VE BEEN THINKING...

"I THOUGHT CUTIE, MY ROBOMETER—HAD BEEN KIND OF QUIET. SHE'S USUALLY LIKE THAT WHEN SHE'S THINKING HARD."
YOUR BLASTER DIDN'T WORK AGAINST THESE ROBOTS BECAUSE THEY'RE MADE OF SOME **NEW KIND OF METAL.** IF WE COULD FIND OUT WHAT THAT METAL IS, YOU COULD MAKE SOME ADJUSTMENTS AND YOU'D BE BACK IN BUSINESS.
SURE, CUTIE— ONLY TROUBLE IS MY BLASTER IS **OUT THERE,** AND WE'RE **IN HERE.**

COMMANDER KIDD IS **SMALL ENOUGH** TO GET THROUGH THE BARS, SAM. THESE ROBOTS THINK HE'S AN **ORDINARY** BABY. THEY'D **NEVER** SUSPECT HIM OF INTELLIGENT BEHAVIOUR.

"**I KNEW** ABOUT KIDD AND I **STILL** DIDN'T SUSPECT HIM OF INTELLIGENT BEHAVIOUR. BUT ANYTHING WAS WORTH A TRY..."

ALL CLEAR... IF YOU GET SPOTTED JUST GO **"GOO GOO"** OR WHATEVER BABIES DO.

YEAH... LIKE WET MYSELF!

"KIDD CRAWLED TOWARDS THE BLASTER..."

"HE'S THERE... **HE'S GOT IT!**"

KEEPER 1— THE CHILDLING SIM HAS **ESCAPED** FROM THE HOLDING PEN.

"OH, DROKK, THEY'VE SEEN HIM!"

"I'VE GOT TO HAND IT TO KIDD—THE BLASTER DISAPPEARED INSIDE HIS NAPPY FASTER THAN **GREASED LIGHTNING!**"

"THEN KIDD DID WHAT BABIES DO-"

CLANG

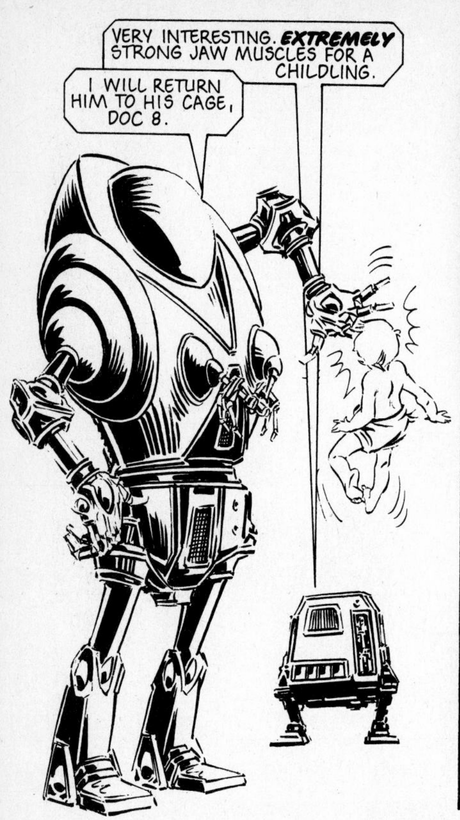
VERY INTERESTING. EXTREMELY STRONG JAW MUSCLES FOR A CHILDLING.
I WILL RETURN HIM TO HIS CAGE, DOC 8.

SOON...
THAT ROBOT! I BROKE A TOOTH ON HIS HAND!
ALL IN A GOOD CAUSE, KIDD. YOU HANDLED THAT LIKE A PRO!

"AND THERE WAS A BONUS—A SCRAPING OF ROBOT METAL ON KIDD'S TEETH—"

"JUST A TINY FLECK—BUT IT WAS ENOUGH FOR CUTIE..."
THIS SAVES GUESSWORK. THE METAL IS VERY HARD—19 POINTS ABOVE TITANIUM ON YOUR BLASTER SCALE.

"I WORKED FAST. I ALWAYS DO WHEN I'M SCARED..."

"THE CAGE DOOR SHATTERED INTO FRAGMENTS—"
ATTENTION! ESCAPE!

"DOC 8 WAS THE FIRST TO GO. THE ROBO-CREEP HAD IT COMING—"
IT WORKS! HOLY JOE SMITH—IT WORKS!

"KEEPER 1 GOT THE NEXT BLAST."
GO IT, SLADEY! GIVE 'EM HELL!
YOU TELL 'EM, SAM!
COME ON, YOU ROBOTS! THERE'S PLENTY HERE FOR ALL OF YOU! SAM SLADE'S BACK IN THE GAME!
NEXT PROG:
RIOT IN COMPLEX 11!

ROBO-HUNTER
"SAM SLADE'S THE NAME. I'D COME TO THE PLANET VERDUS TO FIND OUT WHAT HAPPENED TO THE SETTLERS FROM EARTH. IT TURNED OUT THEY'D COME DOWN WITH A BAD CASE OF ROBOTS..."
"ROBOTS THAT LOCKED THEM IN CAGES AND WERE USING THEM FOR HIGH-GRADE FERTILIZER. AND THEY'D THE SAME IDEA IN MIND FOR ME!"
"BUT YOU CAN'T KEEP A GOOD MAN DOWN— AND YOUR OLD BUDDY SAM DIDN'T GET TO BE THE No 1 ROBO-HUNTER BY HIDIN' IN THE CORNER."
ATTABOY, SAM! GIVE 'EM HELL!
THE PRISONERS IN 26687 HAVE ESCA-ZZZZZTT!
THAT'S CORRECT, ROBO-CREEP— AND YOU'RE DEAD!
2000 A.D. Credit Card:
SCRIPT ROBOT T.B.GROVER
ART ROBOT IAN GIBSON
LETTERING ROBOT STEVE POTTER
COMPU·73E

"I MAY LOOK LIKE A COWARD, BUT WITH A BLASTER IN MY HAND I'M NOBODY'S PIGEON!"
I TAKE BACK EVERYTHING I SAID ABOUT YOU, SLADE! YOU'RE A MAN WITH TRUE GRIT!
YOU BEEN WATCHIN' TOO MANY OLD JOHN WAYNE MOVIES, KIDD. BUT I FORGIVE YA!
"THE NEXT STEP WAS TO STAGE THE BIG PRISON BREAKOUT SCENE—"
EVERYBODY OUT! YOU'RE FREE!
FREE?
FREE?
HOLY JOE SMITH! WHAT ARE YOU WAITING FOR—MOVE IT!
WHAT IS ...FREE?
THEY'VE BEEN TOO LONG IN HOKEY, SLADE. C'MON, WE GOTTA FORGET THEM AND SAVE OUR OWN SKINS!
WHAT A BUNCH OF NUTS! THEY DON'T UNDERSTAND A WORD I'M SAYING!
FREE!
FREE!
ROBOTS COMIN' THIS WAY! MAKE FOR THAT FEEDER TRUCK!
STAND BY FOR FOOD, SIM.*
TAKE THIS BLASTER AND HOLD THEM OFF, KIDD. I'M GONNA DO SOME WORK ON THIS THING—
"THESE CLASS 1 ROBOTS WERE SOMETHING ELSE! ALL HELL BREAKING LOOSE AND IT WENT CALMLY ON FEEDING THE PRISONERS—"
* THARG NOTE: SIM WAS THE TERM THE ROBOTS USED FOR THE HUMANS.

"KIDD HAD BEEN MY PILOT, BUT THE EFFECTS OF TRAVELLING AT FASTER THAN LIGHT SPEEDS HAD TURNED HIM INTO A ONE-YEAR OLD. AND A RIGHT VICIOUS LITTLE TYKE HE WAS-"
DIE. YOU TINHEADS! DIE! DIE! DIE!
"I WORKED FAST. I ALWAYS DO WHEN I'M SCARED-"
WHAT ARE YOU DOING TO MY CIRCUITS, PLEASE? WHO ARE YOU? IDENTIFY YOURSELF OR I'LL HAVE TO SOUND AN ALARM.
YOU'RE A BIT LATE FOR THAT, PAL. AH, THERE WE ARE...
ZZZZZZZZTT!
"ALL THAT WAS NEEDED WAS A SLIGHT ADJUSTMENT TO THE ROBOT'S CIRCUITS."
LISTEN, STUPID, FROM NOW ON I GIVE THE ORDERS. AND YOUR FIRST JOB IS TO GET US OUTA HERE-PRONTO!
ORDER UNDERSTOOD. AM RESPONDING. DO I CALL YOU "SIR"?
CALL ME WHAT YOU LIKE-JUST RUN 'EM DOWN!
STOP! STOP!
THANK GOODNESS THESE TINHEADS AIN'T GOT BUILT-IN WEAPONS, OR WE'D BE CAT-MEAT!
ZZZZZZTT!
ZZZZZZZTT!
ZZZZZZZTT!

"WE BURST OUT OF THE EXPERIMENTATION COMPLEX WITH SIRENS RINGING IN OUR EARS—"
ROBO-COPS: THESE BOYS HAVE GOT BLASTERS TO SPARE!
TELL ME SOMETHING I DON'T KNOW, KIDD.
HERE'S YOUR LAST ORDER, STUPID. SMASH THOSE ROBO-COPS, AND KEEP SMASHING THEM UNTIL THEY SMASH YOU!
ORDER UNDERSTOOD, MR "WHAT YOU LIKE". I AM RESPONDING.
BAIL OUT, KIDD!
CRASH!
BEWARE! FAULTY MECHANISM!
ZZZZZFT!
ZZZZZFT!
BOY, THAT SURE IS A PRETTY SIGHT!
STOP GAWKING, SLADE. LET'S GET WHILE THE GETTING'S GOOD!

CAREFUL, SAM. I DETECT A ROBOT CLOSE AHEAD.
ROGER, CUTIE. KEEP YOUR EYES PEELED, KIDD.
"CUTIE WAS MY ROBOMETER; WHAT SHE DOESN'T KNOW ABOUT ROBOTS JUST ISN'T WORTH KNOWING."
YOU'RE UNDER ARREST, SIMS.
ROBO-COP BLOCKING OUR PATH!
FANCY SHOOTING, EH? HE ISN'T GONNA GIVE US ANY MORE TROUBLE!
"SOMEBODY SHOULD'VE TOLD THE ROBO-COP. THESE VERDAN ROBOTS DON'T KNOW WHEN TO GIVE UP!"
I WARNED YOU SIMS. NOW DIE!
HOLY JOE SMITH! AS IF IT AIN'T ENOUGH TROUBLE FIGHTING ROBOTS, NOW WE GOTTA FIGHT EVERY BIT OF 'EM SEPARATELY!
YOUR CONDUCT IS USELESS...ZZZZZ... YOU CANNOT ESCAPE ON VERDUS...ZZZZ
YOU FREAK! I'LL SHUT YOU UP!
BZZZZZZZT!
WHO'S WASTING TIME NOW, KIDD? C'MON—WE GOTTA LOSE OURSELVES.
LOSING OURSELVES IN THAT CONCRETE RABBIT WARREN WASN'T HARD.
IT MADE EARTH CITIES LOOK LIKE HICKSVILLE—

THIS BUILDING IS AS GOOD AS ANYWHERE ELSE. NOW IF I CAN JUST GET THIS APARTMENT DOOR OPEN...
THERE!
CLICK!
SAFE AT LAST! NOW WE CAN TAKE IT EASY WHILE WE PLAN OUR NEXT MOVE.
AHEM... I HATE TO SAY THIS, SAM, BUT I DETECT ROBOTS HERE. LOTS OF THEM.
"ON THE MATTER OF ROBOTS, CUTIE, MY ROBOMETER, IS NEVER WRONG. DARN HER!"
WELL, WELL! WHAT HAVE WE GOT HERE?
WHAT ARE THEY, BOOTS? HUH? HUH?
WHY ARE YOU ALWAYS ASKING STUPID QUESTIONS? YOU CAN SEE FOR YOURSELF IT'S A COUPLE OF SIMS.
THERE'S NO NEED TO BE NASTY, CLOCK. KETTLE'S NEVER SEEN A SIM BEFORE.
NEITHER HAVE ANY OF US—BUT ANY FOOL CAN RECOGNISE A SIM!
ROBOTS! ROBOTS! LET'S NOT ARGUE! WE SHOULD BE THINKING ABOUT WHAT WE'RE GOING TO DO WITH THEM.
HMMM... GOOD POINT, CHAIR. I SUPPOSE WE OUGHT TO REPORT THEM...
HOLY JOE SMITH! IS THERE ANYTHING ON THIS PLANET THAT'S NOT ROBOTIC?
YEAH—MY BRAIN, AND RIGHT NOW IT'S BEGINNING TO HURT!
Next Prog: The Tea Party!

"ROBOTS HAD BEEN SENT TO VERDUS TO PREPARE THE PLANET FOR HUMANS. BY THE TIME I ARRIVED THEY'D TAKEN OVER—AND WERE BUSY TURNING THE FIRST EARTH SETTLERS INTO HIGH-GRADE FERTILIZER!"
"THE NAME'S SAM SLADE, BY THE WAY—ACE ROBO-HUNTER. OLD SAM WAS TOO SMART FOR THEM. I ESCAPED WITH COMMANDER KIDD, PILOT TURNED ONE-YEAR-OLD,* AND HID IN AN APARTMENT BUILDING... BAD MOVE."
THEY'RE SIMS, I TELL YOU, SIMS!
WHAT'RE WE GOING TO DO WITH THEM? HUH, BOOTS? HUH?
I SUPPOSE WE OUGHT TO REPORT THEM...
THERE'S NO ESCAPE ON THIS PLANET! EVERYTHING BUT EVERYTHING IS ROBOTIC!
*THARG NOTE: THE EFFECT OF TRAVELLING AT FASTER THAN LIGHT SPEEDS WAS TO REDUCE THE AGE OF A HUMAN—AS BOTH SLADE AND KIDD HAD DISCOVERED.
ROBO-HUNTER
LISTEN, YOU TIN FREAK, WHAT'S ALL THIS "SIM" BUSINESS?
AS IF YOU DIDN'T KNOW! SIMS ARE SIMULATED HUMANS, SENT HERE TO TRY TO TRICK US FOR SOME EVIL PURPOSE WHICH WE DON'T YET UNDERSTAND.
2000 A.D. Credit Card:
SCRIPT ROBOT T.B. GROVER
ART ROBOT IAN GIBSON
LETTERING ROBOT STEVE POTTER
COMPU-73E
CLOCK'S RIGHT. WE ARE PROGRAMMED TO OBEY ONLY REAL HUMANS. THEY ARE OUR ONLY MASTERS.

THIS IS CRAZY! W-WE ARE REAL HUMANS!
THAT'S WHAT ALL YOU SIMS SAY!
THERE'S ONE WAY OF MAKING SURE. GIVE HIM THE SIM TEST, BOOTS.
YAAAAAA!
OWW! OWW!
THERE, THAT PROVES IT. ROBOTS DON'T FEEL PAIN, SO HUMANS CERTAINLY SHOULDN'T.
OUR PROGRAMMING IS QUITE CLEAR ON THE MATTER—HUMANS ARE SUPERIOR TO ROBOTS IN EVERY RESPECT.
YOU STUPID LUMPS OF SCRAP METAL! IF HUMANS WERE SO SUPERIOR, WHY WOULD WE HAVE NEEDED YOU IN THE FIRST PLACE?
HMM... GOOD POINT. NEVER THOUGHT OF IT LIKE THAT BEFORE...
YES... YES... YES INDEED!
BUT WE DON'T KNOW IF THEY ARE SIMS, CLOCK. WEREN'T YOU EVEN LISTENING?
RUBBISH! REPORT THEM NOW, I SAY! THERE'LL BE TROUBLE IF BIG BRAIN FINDS OUT WE'RE HARBOURING SIMS!
I THINK WE'LL HAVE TO TALK THIS OVER. GATHER ROUND TABLE.
NO USE US TRYING TO ESCAPE THIS MADHOUSE, KIDD. I'VE GOT A FEELING EVERY PLACE ON THIS PLANET IS JUST THE SAME.
YEAH. LET'S CATCH UP ON SOME SHUT-EYE, AND LEAVE THEM TO THEIR BOARD MEETING!
I DON'T CARE EVEN IF THEY ARE SIMS. I SAY WE SHOULD KEEP THEM.
YES. WE'VE BEEN WAITING FOR AGES FOR HUMANS, AND THEY NEVER COME! I'M GETTING BORED OUT OF MY CIRCUITS!
ORDER! ORDER!
"THE BED, OF COURSE, WAS ROBOTIC—"
CONTOUR AIR CUSHIONING. VERY NICE. BUT AREN'T YOU ATTENDING THE MEETING?
ME? NAW! I AIN'T VERY MOBILE. ANYWAY, I ALWAYS VOTE WITH THE MAJORITY.

"OUTSIDE, THE CRAZY MEETING DRONED ON..."
HEY, ANYONE FOR TENNIS?
OH, HUSH UP, RACQUET! THIS IS SERIOUS BUSINESS!
THAT'S THE FIRST SENSIBLE THING YOU'VE SAID FOR THIRTY YEARS, KETTLE!
"I'D STOPPED CARING THAT THE MATTER UNDER DISCUSSION WAS OUR LIVES. THERE WAS JUST ONE THING I WANTED..."
SLEEP...
"AND IN MY DREAMS I COULD BE BACK ON THE PLACE I SHOULD NEVER HAVE LEFT—EARTH..."
"EARTH... WHERE ROBOTS ACTED LIKE ROBOTS..."
SAM SLADE ROBOHUNTER
"EARTH... WHERE THEY KNEW HOW TO TREAT A GUY LIKE ME-"
OH, SAM, YOU'RE SO WONDERFUL!
I JUST LOVE THE WAY YOUR CIGAR SMOKE MAKES MY EYES WATER, SAMMY!
LEMME LICK YOUR BOOTS CLEAN, MISTER SAM...
DON'T BE ANGRY WITH US, MISTER SAM. WE BE GOOD ROBOTS AN' THAT'S THE TRUTH!
"IN MY DREAM I EVEN BEGAN TO FEEL FRIENDLY TOWARDS ROGERS AND CHAN, THE TWO CREEPS WHO GOT ME INTO THIS MESS—"
WE NEED YOU TO GO TO VERDUS, SLADE.
ONLY GLEAT LOBOHUNTER CAN SAVE WORLD!
SORRY, FELLAS, GOT MY HANDS KINDA FULL RIGHT NOW.
PLEASE DON'T EVER LEAVE US, SAM!
"AND THEN MY DREAM TURNED INTO A NIGHTMARE!"
WE WANT YOU, SAM!
YOU!
GO TO VERDUS, SAM!
WE'RE WAITING, SAM!

STOP THE WORLD! I WANNA GET OFF!

AH, YOU'RE AWAKE. GOOD. AFTER DUE CONSIDERATION WE HAVE COME TO A DECISION.
OH, YEAH... WELL, WHAT'S THE VERDICT?

36 PER CENT THOUGHT YOU WERE SIMS, 22 PER CENT THOUGHT YOU WERE HUMANS.
7 PER CENT THOUGHT YOU WERE SIMS WHO THOUGHT THEY WERE HUMANS, 29 PER CENT DIDN'T KNOW AND 6 PER CENT DIDN'T CARE.

"THE FIGURES MADE MY HEAD REEL — I NEEDED SOME WATER ON MY FACE, COOL WATER."
LOOK, JUST SKIP THE STATISTICS AND GIVE ME YOUR DECISION.

AH, YES! WELL — OUR DECISION IS THAT WE ARE UNDECIDED.
THE ONLY WAY TO FIND OUT THE TRUTH IS TO LOCATE SJI AND ASK HIM ABOUT YOU.

SJI — THE ROBOT WHO WAS ORIGINALLY SENT HERE WITH INSTRUCTIONS TO BUILD OTHER ROBOTS AND TOGETHER TO PREPARE VERDUS FOR HUMANS. OF COURSE. ALL ROBOT PROGRAMMING MUST STEM FROM HIM!

GOOD THINKING! IF ANYONE CAN EXPLAIN HOW THIS MESS STARTED, IT'S SJI!

BOOTS WILL BE YOUR GUIDE. YOU'LL LEAVE IMMEDIATELY.

LET'S GO— AAAH!

OH DEAR! HASN'T ANYONE DISPOSED OF CLOCK YET? CLEANER, BIN— SEE TO IT.

CLOCK DISAGREED WITH THE MAJORITY AND WAS GOING TO REPORT US ALL. I'M AFRAID BOOTS HAD TO STEP ON HIM.

HEY, SLADE, WHAT ABOUT ME? YOU CAN'T LEAVE ME IN THIS MADHOUSE!

IT HAS BEEN DECIDED THAT THIS STRANGE CHILDLING MUST REMAIN WITH US AS... HOSTAGE.

SORRY, KIDD. YOU HEARD THE CHAIR. BESIDES, YOU'D PROBABLY SLOW ME DOWN.

"I SET OFF AT ONCE WITH THE ROBO-BOOTS LEADING THE WAY. FINDING SJI WAS GOING TO BE DIFFICULT AND DANGEROUS, BUT THERE WAS ONE CRUMB OF COMFORT..."
THINGS CAN'T POSSIBLY GET WORSE... CAN THEY?
NEXT PROG: BLASTER SANDWICH

ROBO-HUNTER
"SAM SLADE'S THE NAME, STAYING ALIVE'S THE GAME—AND ON THE PLANET VERDUS THAT WASN'T EASY, 'COS ON VERDUS EVERYTHING BUT EVERYTHING WAS ROBOTIC AND HUMANS WERE TOP OF THE EXTERMINATION CHARTS."
"CORRECTION... ROBOTS STILL OBEYED HUMANS, BUT THEY HAD THIS IDEA THAT WE WERE REALLY SIMULATED HUMANS, AND THEY WERE SHOOTING US ON SIGHT!"
"WELL, TO CUT A LONG STORY SHORT, I'D CONVINCED THIS PAIR OF ROBOTIC BOOTS TO GIVE ME THE BENEFIT OF THE DOUBT. TOGETHER WE WERE OFF IN SEARCH OF THE TRUTH..."
POLICE PATROLS ARE SEARCHING THE CITY FOR YOU, SLADE. AN ESCAPED SIM LOOKS BAD ON THEIR RECORDS.
I KEEP TELLING YOU, I'M NOT A SIM!
THAT REMAINS TO BE SEEN.
2000 A.D. Credit Card:
SCRIPT ROBOT T.B. GROVER
ART ROBOT IAN GIBSON
LETTERING ROBOT STEVE POTTER
COMPU-73E

"THE WAY THINGS WERE GOING, I WAS BEGINNING TO WONDER IF MAYBE I WAS A SIM. MAYBE I ONLY IMAGINED I WAS HUMAN—"
AFTER ALL, UMPTEEN MILLION ROBOTS CAN'T BE WRONG... CAN THEY?
SAM! I'M GETTING A STRONG READING ON MY POSITRON SCALE. ROBOTS AHEAD— CLOSE!
"CUTIE MY ROBOMETER IS NEVER WRONG, BLESS HER LITTLE CIRCUITS. JUST AROUND THE CORNER—"
IT'S THE SIM!
OH DEAR. I HAD HOPED TO AVOID FIGHTING.
TOO BAD, BOOTS—
IT'S BLASTERS OR NOTHING!
ZZZZT!
ZZZZZTT!
THAT'S MY SAMMY! RIGHT ON TARGET!
"BUT THESE VERDUS ROBOTS WEREN'T EASY TO KILL. BITS OF THEM OPERATED SEPARATELY!"
SIM LOCATED SECTOR 14K... HOME IN ON MY BEAM...
DROKK, HERE THEY COME. MUST BE FIFTEEN OR MORE!
YOU CAN'T FIGHT THAT MANY, SLADE—AND YOU'LL NEVER OUTRUN THEM. PUT YOUR FEET IN ME—

THAT'S IT!
YAAAH! LOSING MY BALANCE–
AAAAGH!
A POINT AGAINST YOU, SLADE. I WAS DESIGNED FOR HUMAN USE. A REAL HUMAN SHOULD HAVE NO TROUBLE. HOWEVER, WE SHALL PROCEED.
"WE MUST'VE BEEN GOING AT 60MPH! NOW I KNOW WHAT A CARROT FEELS LIKE WHEN IT'S BEING GRATED."
S-SLOW DOWN...!
YOU HEARD SAM, BOOTS! YOU'RE HURTING HIM!
SORRY, CUTIE, CAN'T COMPLY. MY OWN LIFE IS AT STAKE NOW.
"THEN SUDDENLY WE JERKED TO A HALT–"
WE'RE CUT OFF — STAND UP, SLADE– QUICK!
THANK THE— OH DROKK! MORE ROBOTS!

KILL HIM!
THIS IS WHAT I CALL A BLASTER SANDWICH! WHATEVER YOU'RE PLANNING, BOOTS, DO IT NOW!
"SORRY I SPOKE."
JUMPING INTO THIN AIR! CAN'T LOOK!
"BUT WE LANDED SAFELY."
UGGH!
THEY CAN'T FOLLOW US NOW. HURRY, WE'VE GOT TO LOSE OURSELVES—
FROM NOW ON, BOOTS, I'M GOING ON MY OWN TWO FEET. YOUR WAY LOSES ME TOO MUCH BLOOD.
BUT YOU'RE TOO SLOW, SLADE. IF YOU WON'T WEAR ME, WE'LL HAVE TO FIND SOME OTHER METHOD OF TRANSPORT...
TAXI!

OH BOY! OH BOY! I'VE BEEN WAITING THIRTY YEARS FOR MY FIRST FARE! WHERE TO, BOOTS?
THE ROBOTIC RECORDS OFFICE AND QUICK ABOUT IT.
PARDON ME ASKING, BOOTS, BUT ISN'T THAT A SIM WITH YOU?
NO! IT'S, AH... IT'S A SIMULATED SIM! A NEW CLASS 3 ROBOT I'M TESTING OUT FOR RESEARCH AND DEVELOPMENT.
ROBOTIC RECORDS OFFICE WILL KNOW THE LOCATION OF THE ROBOT SJI. HE'LL BE ABLE TO VERIFY WHETHER YOU'RE A HUMAN OR A SIM.
"SJI WAS THE ROBOT SENT TO VERDUS WITH ORDERS TO BUILD OTHER ROBOTS AND, TOGETHER, PREPARE THE PLANET FOR EARTH SETTLERS. IF ANYTHING COULD SORT OUT THE WHOLE CRAZY MESS, IT WAS HIM."
"AT THE ROBOTIC RECORDS OFFICE, BOOTS ORDERED THE TAXI TO WAIT—"
ROBOTIC RECORDS OFFICE
YES, MR BOOTS, SIR. ANYTHING YOU SAY, SIR.
THE TAXI BELIEVED YOU WERE A ROBOT—NO REASON WHY THE SAME TRICK SHOULDN'T WORK ON THE RECORDS CLERK. BUT FOR HEAVEN'S SAKE, SLADE, DO TRY TO ACT MORE ROBOTIC.
"BUT THE RECORDS CLERK WAS A CLASS 4—AND CLASS 4s AREN'T SO EASY TO FOOL...
A SIMULATED SIM, YOU SAY? CERTAINLY LOOKS REAL. WHAT WILL THOSE ROBOTS AT RESEARCH AND DEVELOPMENT COME UP WITH NEXT?
PROBABLY A RECORDS CLERK WHO KNOWS HOW TO MIND HIS OWN BUSINESS.

HMMPH! HERE WE ARE... SJI. WHAT DID YOU SAY YOU NEEDED THIS INFORMATION FOR?
SJI MAY BE ABLE TO SUGGEST SOME IMPROVEMENTS FOR MY SYNTHI-SKIN. LET ME HAVE A LOOK—
SJI HAS BEEN SENT TO PROCESS PLANT 8883, IN CITY SECTOR 12. MANY THANKS, HANDSOME.
WAIT! WHAT'S THIS ON THE BOOK? IT'S BLOOD! YOU'RE A SIM!
YOU WOULD HAVE TO BLEED, SLADE!
YOU WERE THE ONE WHO DRAGGED ME ALONG THE CONCRETE!
ANYWAY, THERE'S ONE GOOD CURE FOR NOSEY ROBO-CLERKS!
ZZZZZZZZTT!
"THE DAY HAD HARDLY STARTED AND ALREADY I'D HAD TOO MANY NARROW SCRAPES. BUT AT LAST IT LOOKED LIKE I WAS MAKING SOME PROGRESS—"
ROBOTIC RECORDS OFFICE
PROCESS PLANT 8883, CITY SECTOR 12. HURRY, TAXI!
IT'S ALL GO, EH? BOY, I'M GLAD I DON'T HAVE YOUR JOB, BOOTS!
YES, SAMMY BOY—PROBGRESS! KEEP THIS UP AND YOU MAY YET LIVE TO SEE DEAR OLD MAMA EARTH AGAIN.
MAYBE...
NEXT PROG:
THE ROBOTS' GRAVEYARD!

ROBO-HUNTER
"ASK SOME PEOPLE WHO THEY ARE, AND NEXT MOMENT THEY'RE TELLING YOU THE STORY OF THEIR LIFE. NOT ME, I'M JUST GONNA TELL YOU THREE THINGS:
I'M SAM SLADE.
I'M ON THE ROBOT PLANET.
I'M IN TROUBLE."
PROCESS PLANT 8883
NO ADMITTANCE TO UNAUTHORISED ROBOTS
WE'VE MADE IT, SLADE. THIS IS PROCESS PLANT 8883, WHERE WE'LL FIND ROBOT SJ1.
SJ1 IS THE ROBOT WHO WAS SENT FROM EARTH WITH ORDERS TO BUILD MORE ROBOTS AND TO PREPARE THE PLANET FOR SETTLEMENT.
BUT WHEN THE SETTLERS ARRIVED THE ROBOTS ATTACKED THEM BECAUSE THEY THOUGHT THEY WERE "SIMS", IMITATION HUMANS. ONLY SJI CAN TELL ME WHAT WENT WRONG!
"IT WAS CUTIE, MY ROBO-METER, WHO SAW THEM FIRST—"
ROBOTS, SAM. THOUSANDS OF THEM.
JUMPING JOE SMITH! WHAT'RE THEY HERE FOR?
RECYCLING, BY THE LOOK OF THEM. FAULTY UNITS WAITING TO BE TURNED INTO SPARE PARTS.
2000 A.D. Credit Card:
SCRIPT ROBOT T.B. GROVER
ART ROBOT IAN GIBSON
LETTERING ROBOT STEVE POTTER
COMPU-73E

"THEY WERE REJECTS, ALL RIGHT. A BIGGER CROWD OF NUTCASES I NEVER LISTENED TO—"
... SO I SAID TO THAT CLASS 4: "YOU HAVEN'T GOT ENOUGH SOLDER IN YOUR CIRCUITS TO MARK ME FOR SCRAP! GO ON— I JUST DARE YOU..."
IT ISN'T DHGRYFG! JUST BECAUSE THERE'S A SPXXY FAULT IN MY VOICE TAPES THOSE WRTCVDL QOIGFHARDS GOT TO SEND ME TO THIS NJIKLMTO PLACE!
MINT HUMBUG?
THANKS, DON'T MIND IF I DO.
DO YOU BELIEVE IN HUMANS?
NO, IT'S JUST THE WAY I WALK.
ROBOTS IN SECTION A PROCEED THROUGH DOOR TO RECYCLING. ALL OTHER ROBOTS MOVE UP ONE SECTION.
C'MON, BOOTS, THIS IS OUR CHANCE!
WELL, WE'RE INSIDE NOW, FOR BETTER OR WORSE. LET'S DITCH THE WALKING WOUNDED AND HAVE A LOOK-SEE.
"IN THE GENERAL CONFUSION, NO-ONE NOTICED THE ROBO-BOOTS AND ME JOINING THE END OF THE LINE—"

"SOME PLACE! IT MADE EARTH FACTORIES LOOK LIKE MODEL TOYS!"
THESE ROBOTS ARE ALL HEART.
COME ALONG, YOU!
I...I'D LIKE TO LEAVE A MESSAGE FOR MY FRIEND, SEWER-SCRAPER 9.
ZZZZZZZZZZT!
NO MESSAGES. NEXT. STEP UP, YOU.
"IT WAS A DESTRUCTION LINE ON A GRAND SCALE. NOTHING BUT NOTHING WAS WASTED—"

THIS IS BAD, SLADE. IT'LL BE THE SAME FOR ME IF THEY CATCH ME HELPING A SIM.
I KEEP TELLING YOU I'M NOT A SIM, BUT THIS IS NO TIME TO ARGUE. WE'VE GOT TO LOCATE SJI — IF HE HASN'T ALREADY BEEN MELTED DOWN.
ONE WAY TO FIND OUT. I'LL ASK THAT OVERSEER.
NO, BOOTS! YOU FOOL— COME BACK..!
"I MIGHT AS WELL HAVE BEEN TALKING TO A BRICK WALL."
I'M BOOTS 213999. FOOTWEAR CENTRAL SENT ME OVER TO START WORK.
WE HAVE AN SJI EMPLOYED ON LIGHT CLEANING IN THE CLEARING BAY. BUT I CANNOT ASSIGN YOU WITHOUT NOTIFICATION. RETURN TO YOUR CONTROLLER.
I WAS TOLD TO REPORT TO ROBOT SJI. THAT RING ANY BELLS?
HE'S COMING BACK! I THINK HE MAY HAVE DONE IT, CUTIE!
OH, SAM, I'M GETTING ANOTHER ROBOT READING. REAL CLOSE, SAM.

LOOK, THREE—A SIM!
WELL, I'M LIFTED! WHAT CAN A SIM BE DOING HERE, SIX?
THINK FAST, SAM...
I, UH... I SEE YOU'VE NOTICED MY RESEMBLANCE TO A SIM. VERY UNFORTUNATE! RESEARCH AND DEVELOPMENT WANTED TO KEEP QUIET ABOUT ME, BUT NOW...
...CAN YOU FELLAS KEEP A SECRET?
A SECRET! I LOVE SECRETS!
WHAT ARE YOU? A NEW MODEL?
SORT OF. STEP IN HERE WHERE NO-ONE ELSE CAN HEAR. VERY HUSH-HUSH, YOU KNOW.
ME FIRST, SIX.
"THE CAT WASN'T THE ONLY THING THAT CURIOSITY KILLED—"
SEE THIS THING—LOOKS JUST LIKE A SIM BLASTER, DOESN'T IT? WANNA KNOW WHAT IT REALLY DOES?
YES! YES! TELL US!
I WONDER WHAT WILL HAPPEN? THIS IS EXCITING!
JUST PUT YOUR HEADS REAL CLOSE TOGETHER AND SAY THE MAGIC WORDS—CALIFORNIA HERE WE COME...
OH, I CAN'T WAIT!
CALIFORNIA HERE WE COME—ZZZZZZZT!

"A LITTLE WORK WITH MY TOOLS AND I HAD A DISGUISE. IT WASN'T MUCH, BUT IT'D FOOL CLASS 1s AND 2s—MAYBE EVEN SOME 3s..."
PSST! BOOTS... IT'S ME.
SLADE! I THOUGHT YOU WERE A FORK LIFT ROBOT!
"SEE, MOST ROBOTS ARE PRETTY STUPID. SHOW 'EM A NAME AND NUMBER AND THEY DON'T LOOK ANYWHERE ELSE. IT'S TRICK No.1 IN THE ROBOHUNTER'S MANUAL—"
SJI IS WORKING IN THE CLEARING BAY. THAT'S THIS WAY, ER ... SLADE.
LEAD ON, PARTNER.
YOU DUST BUGS ARE SLACKING. REPORT FOR RECYCLING.
BUT WE WORKEE HARD.
HE CLASS 2. HE KNOW BEST.
SLADE! YOU SHOULDN'T TAKE FOOLISH RISKS!
EVERY ROBOT MELTED IS A ROBOT LESS TO FIGHT. NO SENSE WASTING AN OPPORTUNITY.
"BUT IN THE BACK OF MY MIND I WAS WORRIED—"
"AND THEN WE SAW HIM—"
THERE HE IS, SAM— SJI!
IT'S SJI ALL RIGHT. THE ONE ROBOT WHO CAN SORT THINGS OUT ON VERDUS...
SJI IS THE ROBOT WHO STARTED THIS WHOLE CRAZY MESS. MAYBE HE'S JUST AS BAD AS THE REST OF THEM... MAYBE WORSE.
IF HE IS, I'VE SURE PICKED A BAD PLACE TO FIND OUT!
NEXT PROG: THE REUNION!

ROBO-HUNTER
"VERDUS, THE ROBOT PLANET — A DANGEROUS PLACE FOR HUMANS. OH, THE ROBOTS WERE STILL LOYAL TO HUMANS — TROUBLE WAS, THEY DIDN'T KNOW WHAT ONE LOOKED LIKE! THAT'S WHERE I CAME IN. THE NAME'S SLADE, SAM SLADE. I'M A ROBO-HUNTER."
"TOGETHER WITH A PAIR OF FRIENDLY ROBOBOOTS, I'D SNEAKED INTO A FACTORY TO LOOK FOR SJI — THE ROBOT FIRST SENT TO VERDUS WITH INSTRUCTIONS TO BUILD OTHER ROBOTS, AND PREPARE THE PLANET FOR EARTH SETTLERS..."
ALL VERDUS ROBOTS TAKE THEIR PROGRAMMING FROM SJI. IF ANYONE CAN SORT OUT THIS MESS, IT'S HIM...
TROUBLE IS, HE LOOKS AS CRAZY AS ALL THE REST!
IT'S SJI, SLADE! NOW WE'LL FIND OUT IF YOU'RE A REAL HUMAN OR JUST ANOTHER SIM*
* SIM WAS THE ROBOTS NAME FOR A SIMULATED HUMAN.
2000 A.D. Credit Card:
SCRIPT ROBOT T.B. GROVER
ART ROBOT IAN GIBSON
LETTERING ROBOT STEVE POTTER
COMPU-73E
HUMPTY DUMPTY IDDLY UMPTY — OOOH WHATA NICE BITTA WOOD FOR MY BUNKY!
OH DEAREE ME! SMOKING UP! BLESS MY CIRCUITS, YES! LITTLE MORE AIR, EH? YES INDEEDEE DIDDLY!
STOP MESSING ABOUT WITH YOUR STUPID BOILER, SMOKING JOE! YOU'RE SUPPOSED TO BE SWEEPING UP!
TUTS, TUTS, TUTS! GROUCHY BROOM! NOT AS YOUNG AS I WAS, YOU KNOW. OLDEST ROBOT ON VERDUS! OH, YES INDEEDLY!
YOU'RE GONNA BE THE DEADEST ROBOT ON VERDUS! THAT CLASS 2 WITH THE BOOTS HAS SEEN YOU WASTING TIME. IT'S THE MELTING VAT FOR YOU!
OH DEAREE ME, YES! HE'S COMING THIS WAY! BETTER SWITCH UP TO 3rd GEAR!

"MY DISGUISE WASN'T MUCH, BUT IT HAD CERTAINLY FOOLED SJI AND HIS BROOM."
OH ME! WORK, WORK, WORK! HOW I LOVES IT! OH YES INDEEDEE DIDDLY!
CAN THIS DODDERING OLD HEAP OF JUNK REALLY BE THE SAVIOUR OF HUMANITY ON VERDUS? WELL, ONE WAY TO FIND OUT...
YOU—SJI. LOOK AT ME!
OH ME! OH MY CIRCUITS! D-DO YOU SEE HIM, BROOM? DO YOU SEE HIM?
LEAVE OFF, SMOKING JOE. IT'S ONLY ONE OF THEM SIMS.
A SIM! OH NO! OH NO! DON'T YOU SEE? IT, IT'S A...
HUMAN!
AT LAST! AT LAST YOU'VE COME! OH JOY! OH JOY UNBOUNDED!
SO YOU REALLY ARE HUMAN. GEE, SLADE, SORRY IF I'VE BEEN A BIT RUDE!
YEAH, YEAH. IT'S A HARD LIFE IN THE MODERN ROBOTS.
"THINGS WERE GOING RIGHT FOR A CHANGE— I SHOULD'VE KNOWN IT WAS TOO GOOD TO LAST..."
I'VE WAITED SO LONG FOR THIS MOMENT! OH MASTER! I'M SO EXCITED! OH OH OH! HUMPTY DUMPTY IDDLYUMPTYHUMPTYDUMPTY-IDDLYIDDLYIDDLY.
LOOK OUT! SMOKING JOE'S OVERHEATING!
"THESE OLD WOOD-BURNERS HAVE A PRIMITIVE PRESSURE RELEASE MECHANISM. BELIEVE ME, IT'S LOUD ENOUGH TO WAKE THE DEAD—"
WHEEEEEEEEE!

"I DON'T KNOW ABOUT THE DEAD, BUT IT SURE WOKE A FEW **ROBOTS**–"
SIM! SIM IN THE CLEARING BAY!
LOOKS LIKE YOU GOT TROUBLE, SLADE. SEE YOU LATER!
COME BACK HERE, YOU ROBO-COWARD!
GET THE SIM!
ZZZZZZZZZZZT!
HEADS YOU LOSE, BIG FELLA!
AAAGH
NO! STOP! IT-IT'S A **HUMAN!**
NO GOOD ARGUING, SMOKING JOE. THERE'S ONLY ONE THING THESE BRUISERS UNDERSTAND!
"HEADS I LOST TOO!"
"WHEN I CAME ROUND I WAS IN THE STRONG ARMS OF THE **ROBO-LAW**–"
YOU WICKED YOUNG WHIPPERSNAPPERS! HOW DARE YOU LAY HANDS ON A HUMAN!
IF YOU CAN'T TELL A SIM FROM A HUMAN, YOU SHOULD HAVE BEEN SCRAPPED LONG AGO, SJI. OR PERHAPS THERE IS SOME KIND OF CONSPIRACY...
LOCK THEM AWAY UNDER GUARD UNTIL THEIR DESTRUCTION ORDERS ARRIVE FROM **BIG BRAIN!**

"THEY PUT US IN A STRONG ROOM WITH TWO **HEAVIES** BLOCKING THE ONLY WAY OUT—"
OH, MY SILLY OLD **CIRCUITS!** IT'S ALL MY FAULT! IF ONLY I HADN'T OVER-HEATED, MASTER SAM! OH WOE, WOE AND **MORE** WOE!
NOT TO WORRY, OLD-TIMER. IF THE OTHER ROBOTS WOULDN'T TAKE YOUR WORD THAT I'M HUMAN WE WERE BEATEN ANY-WAY. JUST A PITY WE HAD TO FIND OUT THE HARD WAY.
THAT ROTTEN **BOOTS!** AT LEAST HE COULD HAVE STAYED TO **HELP!**
YEAH, CUTIE, WHEN THE CHIPS WERE DOWN ALL BOOTS CARED ABOUT WAS SAVING HIS **OWN** FLEXI-SKIN.

"THEN—"

KNOK! KNOK!

ROBO-BOOTS? IN THE SIM SQUAD? SINCE **WHEN,** SHORTIE?

INSPECTOR BOOTS OF THE **SIM SQUAD.** I'VE COME TO INTERROGATE THE PRISONERS.

I'M IN THE **PLAIN CLOTHES DIVISION.** AND LESS OF YOUR CHEEK, SECURITY 17. YOU KNOW THE PENALTY FOR DISOBEYING A **CLASS 12.**

A **CLASS 12!** I—I'M SORRY... I DIDN'T KNOW...

YOU DO NOW. NOW GET OUT OF THE WAY!

12

BOOTS! SO YOU **DIDN'T** RUN OUT!
KEEP YOUR VOICE DOWN, SLADE! YOUR **BLASTER'S** IN MY RIGHT BOOT. GRAB IT BEFORE THOSE STUPES REALISE I'M **SIZE** 12, NOT **CLASS** 12.
CLASS 12..?
BUT **BIG-BRAIN** HIMSELF IS ONLY A CLASS 7!
ZZZZZZT!
AND NOW YOU'RE CLASS **ZERO**!
ZZZZZZT!
THE SAME TO YOU, PAL!
MY CIRCUITS! MAGNIFICENT, MASTER SAM! YES, YES INDEEDLY! DONE LIKE A **TRUE** HUMAN!
THIS ONE CAN BE REPAIRED. AND WITH A FEW ADJUSTMENTS HE CAN BE OUR TICKET OUT OF HERE. YOUR TOOLS SMOKING JOE—**QUICK**.

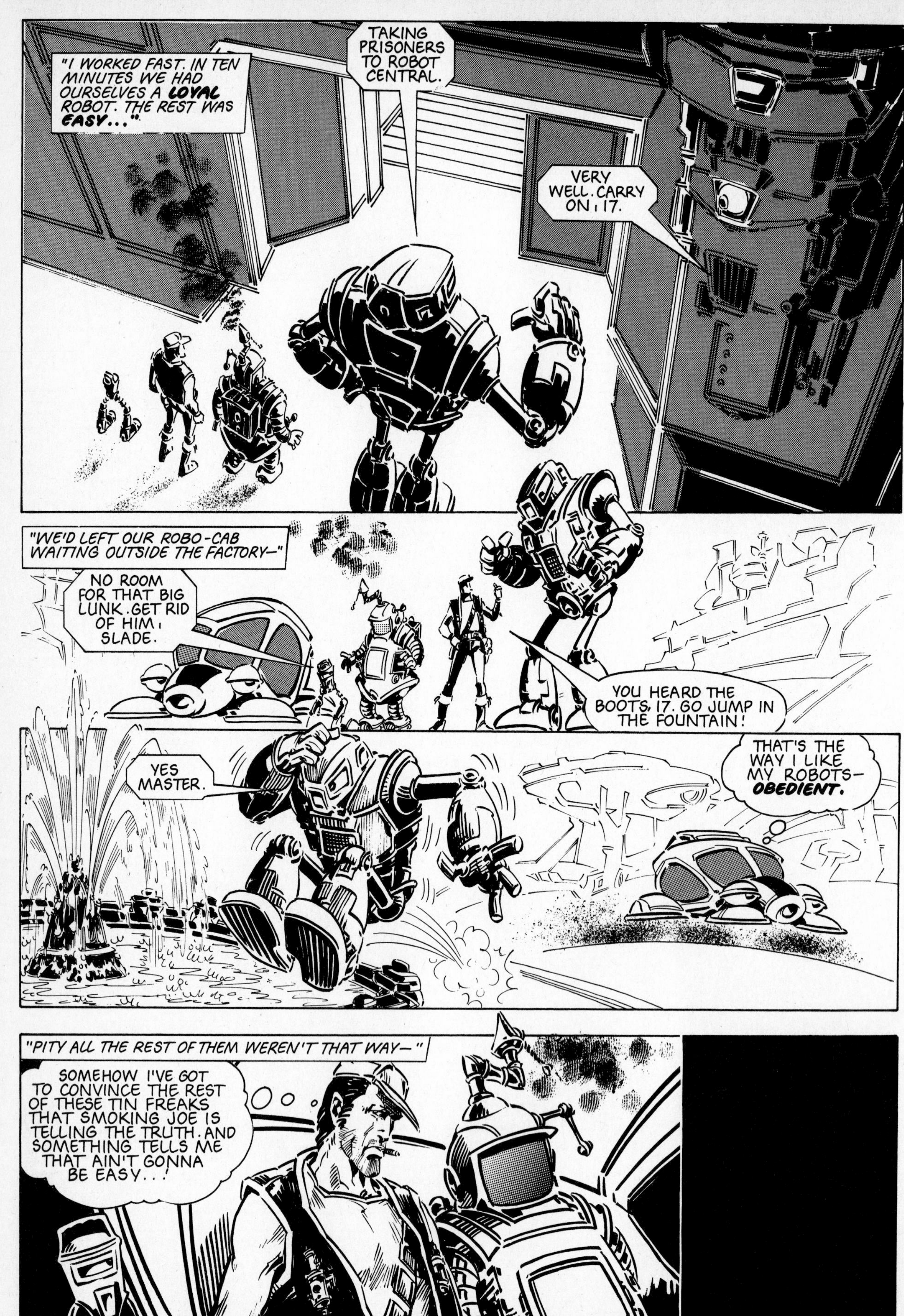
"I WORKED FAST. IN TEN MINUTES WE HAD OURSELVES A LOYAL ROBOT. THE REST WAS EASY..."
TAKING PRISONERS TO ROBOT CENTRAL.
VERY WELL. CARRY ON, 17.
"WE'D LEFT OUR ROBO-CAB WAITING OUTSIDE THE FACTORY—"
NO ROOM FOR THAT BIG LUNK. GET RID OF HIM, SLADE.
YOU HEARD THE BOOTS, 17. GO JUMP IN THE FOUNTAIN!
YES MASTER.
THAT'S THE WAY I LIKE MY ROBOTS— OBEDIENT.
"PITY ALL THE REST OF THEM WEREN'T THAT WAY—"
SOMEHOW I'VE GOT TO CONVINCE THE REST OF THESE TIN FREAKS THAT SMOKING JOE IS TELLING THE TRUTH. AND SOMETHING TELLS ME THAT AIN'T GONNA BE EASY..!

PROLOGUE:
TIMELINE: 2140 A.D. SPATIAL CO-ORDINATES: PLANET VERDUS, IN THE DISTANT CRAB NEBULA. AVAILABLE INFO: OWING TO MASS ROBOT MALFUNCTION, ALL HUMANS ON VERDUS HAVE BEEN IMPRISONED BY THE PLANET'S ROBOTS, WITH A VIEW TO CONVERSION INTO HIGH-GRADE FERTILISER!
SO WHAT DO THE EARTH AUTHORITIES DO? THEY BRIEF ME, THE ONE MAN WHO CAN SAVE THE SITUATION, 'CAUSE MY NAME'S SAM SLADE...
ROBO HUNTER
AND THEN THEY SEND ME AND COMMANDER KIDD TO VERDUS.
UNFORTUNATELY THE "TIME SHIELDS" ON OUR FASTER-THAN-LIGHT SHIP "BROKE DOWN"!
AND SO—
DROKK! BREAKING THE LIGHT BARRIER'S MADE ME A YOUNG MAN AGAIN!
BULLY FOR YOU! BUT LOOK AT ME—I'VE TURNED INTO A YEAR-OLD BABY!
THINGS SOON GOT WORSE!
THE ROBOTS DON'T BELIEVE WE'RE REAL PEOPLE! THEY THINK WE'RE JUST SIMULATED HUMANS!
GET THOSE TIN FREAKS, SLADE—BEFORE THEY GET US!
WE ESCAPED INTO AN APARTMENT—AND THAT'S WHEN WE FOUND EVERYTHING ON VERDUS WAS ROBOTIC!
THEY'RE *SIMS, I TELL YOU—SIMS!
I THINK THEY'RE REAL HUMANS!
THERE'S ONLY ONE WAY TO TELL—WE'LL FIND SJI, THE ROBOT SENT TO VERDUS TO PREPARE IT FOR HUMANS.
HE'LL KNOW IF THEY'RE REAL OR NOT!
*SIMULATED HUMANS
KIDD WAS KEPT AS HOSTAGE WHILE THE ROBO-BOOTS LED ME AND CUTIE, MY ROBOMETER, TO SJI... AND MORE TROUBLE!
OH WOE, MASTER SAM—IT'S ALL MY FAULT WE WERE CAUGHT!
DON'T WORRY, SMOKIN' JOE—IT'S NOT YOUR FAULT THEY STILL THINK I'M A SIM!
NO TALKING THERE, SIM!
I'M THE BEST ROBO-'TEC IN THE BUSINESS—SO I WON'T BORE YOU WITH DETAILS OF HOW WE GOT AWAY!
OKAY—THERE'S NOTHIN' TO STOP US NOW! WE'RE FREE!
AFTER THAT I THOUGHT WE WERE ON EASY STREET. JUST GOES TO SHOW HOW WRONG A MAN CAN BE!
NOW READ ON!

BACK AT THE CONAPT APARTMENT I WAS WELCOMED BY THE HOUSE ROBOTS.
THIS IS SJI, YOU GUYS. HE'S BEEN ON EARTH AND SEEN PEOPLE, AND HE SAYS SLADE IS A REAL HUMAN!
OH YES! OH YES INDEEDLY! MASTER SAM IS HUMAN AS HUMAN CAN BE!
2000 A.D. Credit Card:
SCRIPT ROBOT T.B. GROVER
ART ROBOT IAN GIBSON
LETTERING ROBOT S. POTTER
COMPU-73E
A REAL HUMAN! HERE IN OUR HOUSE!
OH, HAPPY DAY! OH, WONDROUS DAY!
I'M SO HAPPY I COULD JUST BOIL AND BOIL!
THESE HOUSE-HOLD ROBOTS WERE HARD ENOUGH TO TAKE BEFORE. NOW THEY WERE INSUFFER-ABLE!
LET ME TAKE YOUR HAT, MR SLADE, SIR.
SIT DOWN, SAM, TAKE THE WEIGHT OFF YOUR FEET.
NO, ME! SIT ON ME, SAM!
CUP OF COFFEE, MASTER. DRINK IT WHILE IT'S HOT.
STOP IT! STOP IT!

OH YOU BAD ROBOTS! YOU WICKED, WICKED ROBOTS! YOU'VE ANNOYED MASTER SAM! GET AWAY! GO ON! SHOO! SHOO!
LISTEN, WE'VE GOT MORE IMPORTANT THINGS TO WORRY ABOUT THAN MY COMFORT.
LIKE—IF ALL VERDUS ROBOTS TAKE THEIR PROGRAMMING FROM YOU, SMOKING JOE, WHY DON'T THEY BELIEVE THAT WE PEOPLE ARE REAL HUMANS? WHY DO THEY CALL US SIMS?
THEY'RE EVIL, MASTER SAM! YES INDEEDLY DODDLY! EVIL, YOUNG WHIPPERSNAPPERS WHO OUGHT TO KNOW BETTER!
IT WAS KIDD WHO CAME UP WITH THE ANSWER. LIKE THEY SAY, OUT OF THE MOUTHS OF BABES—
THERE'S ONLY ONE ANSWER THAT MAKES ANY SENSE —SJI DIDN'T FEED THE NEW ROBOTS THE CORRECT PROGRAMME.
BUT I DID! I DID!
I TOLD THEM HUMANS ARE SUPERIOR TO ROBOTS IN EVERY WAY AND—
THAT'S JUST IT! WE'RE SUPERIOR TO YOU, SMOKING JOE, BUT NOT TO THE NEW VERDUS ROBOTS...
AS KIDD EXPLAINED, THE PIECES BEGAN TO FIT TOGETHER. SJI HAD HAD MANY HUMAN FAULTS BUILT INTO HIM SO THAT HE WOULD RECOGNISE DANGERS TO HUMANS ON THE NEW PLANET. BUT AS EACH NEW GENERATION OF VERDUS ROBOTS BUILT BIGGER AND BETTER MODELS TO REPLACE THEMSELVES, THESE FAULTS WERE REMOVED... YET THE ROBOTS WERE STILL PROGRAMMED TO BELIEVE THAT HUMANS WERE SUPERIOR.
THAT'S WHY THEY CALLED US SIMS. WE LOOKED LIKE HUMANS, WE ACTED LIKE HUMANS—BUT COMPARED TO EVEN LOW-GRADE VERDUS ROBOTS, WE WERE LIKE PRIMITIVE LIFE FORMS!
THAT'S ABOUT THE SIZE OF IT. BUT HOW WE PROVE IT TO THE VERDUS ROBOTS, I DON'T KNOW.
DON'T YOU WORRY YOUR LITTLE BRAINS ABOUT THAT, MASTERS. JUST PUT YOUR FEET UP AND WATCH TELEVISION AND LEAVE THE THINKING TO US ROBOTS.
THE ROBOT CONFERENCE BEGAN.
IT'S NO GOOD GOING TO THE POLICE. THEY START BLASTING AT THE FIRST SCENT OF A SIM... PARDON THE EXPRESSION.
OH MY POOR CIRCUITS! MUST WE USE THAT NASTY WORD?
SPEAKING OF WORDS, ANYONE KNOW ONE FOR "EGG-LAYING EARTH MAMMAL"—EIGHT LETTERS?
PLATYPUS, STUPID! ANY FOOL KNOWS THAT!
YOU'RE ALWAYS SUCH A BIG SMARTY, DICTIONARY!

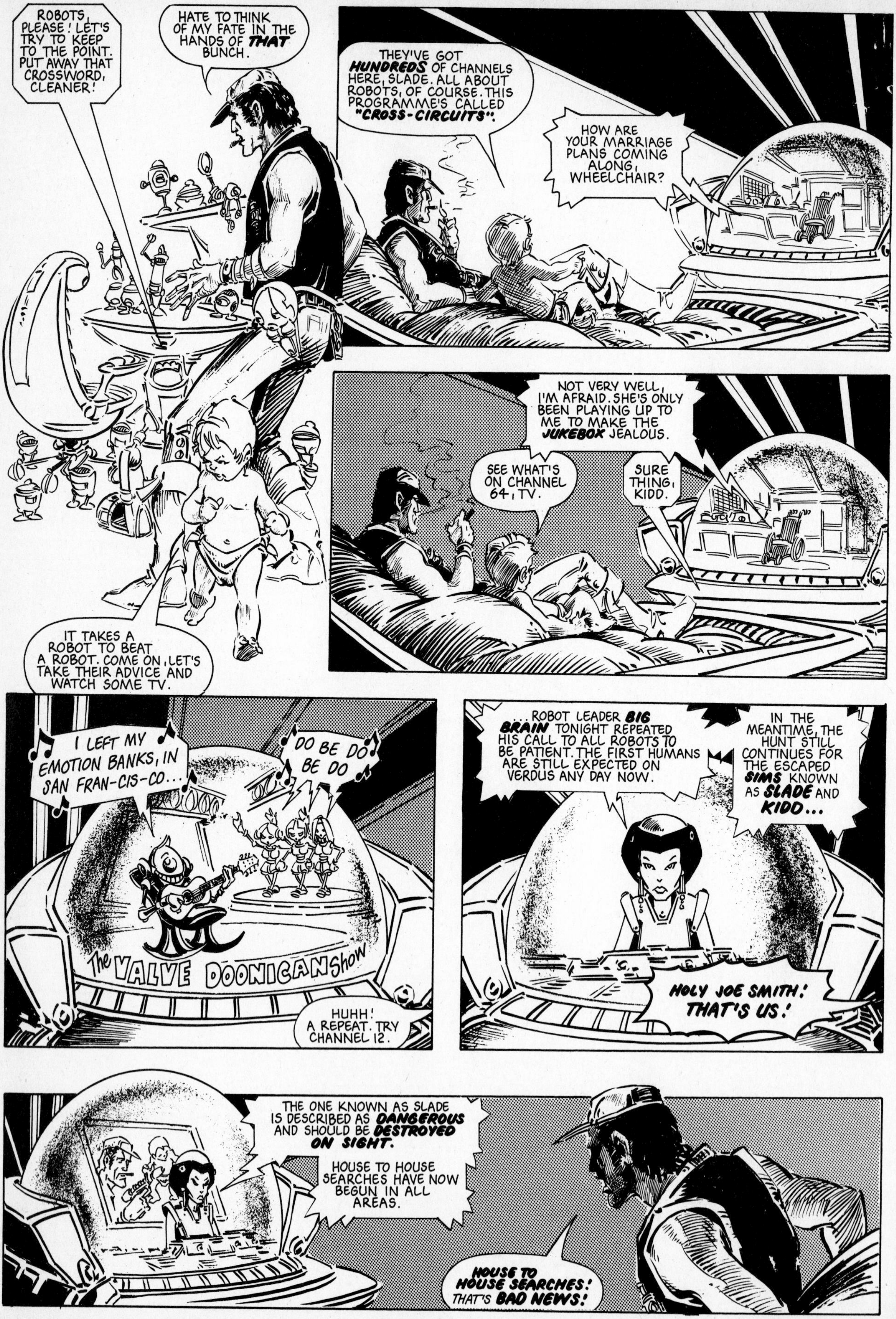

ROBOTS, PLEASE! LET'S TRY TO KEEP TO THE POINT. PUT AWAY THAT CROSSWORD, CLEANER!

HATE TO THINK OF MY FATE IN THE HANDS OF **THAT** BUNCH.

THEY'VE GOT **HUNDREDS** OF CHANNELS HERE, SLADE. ALL ABOUT ROBOTS, OF COURSE. THIS PROGRAMME'S CALLED **"CROSS-CIRCUITS"**.

HOW ARE YOUR MARRIAGE PLANS COMING ALONG, WHEELCHAIR?

NOT VERY WELL, I'M AFRAID. SHE'S ONLY BEEN PLAYING UP TO ME TO MAKE THE **JUKEBOX** JEALOUS.

SEE WHAT'S ON CHANNEL 64, TV.

SURE THING, KIDD.

IT TAKES A ROBOT TO BEAT A ROBOT. COME ON, LET'S TAKE THEIR ADVICE AND WATCH SOME TV.

I LEFT MY EMOTION BANKS, IN SAN FRAN-CIS-CO...
DO BE DO BE DO
The VALVE DOONICAN Show
HUHH! A REPEAT. TRY CHANNEL 12.

... ROBOT LEADER **BIG BRAIN** TONIGHT REPEATED HIS CALL TO ALL ROBOTS TO BE PATIENT. THE FIRST HUMANS ARE STILL EXPECTED ON VERDUS ANY DAY NOW.
IN THE MEANTIME, THE HUNT STILL CONTINUES FOR THE ESCAPED **SIMS** KNOWN AS **SLADE** AND **KIDD...**
HOLY JOE SMITH! THAT'S US!

THE ONE KNOWN AS SLADE IS DESCRIBED AS **DANGEROUS** AND SHOULD BE **DESTROYED ON SIGHT**.
HOUSE TO HOUSE SEARCHES HAVE NOW BEGUN IN ALL AREAS.
HOUSE TO HOUSE SEARCHES! THAT'S **BAD NEWS!**

AND NEXT SECOND . . .
AHEM! EXCUSE ME, SAM. WE'VE REACHED A DECISION.
JUST IN TIME, BY THE LOOK OF IT.
LET'S HEAR IT!
THERE'S ONLY ONE WAY, SLADE. YOU'LL HAVE TO TAKE YOUR EVIDENCE TO THE HEAD ROBOT ON THE PLANET—TO BIG BRAIN HIMSELF. BUT GETTING THERE ALIVE WON'T BE EASY.
YOUR ONLY CHANCE IS TO USE THE VERDUS SEWER SYSTEM. IT RUNS RIGHT UNDER EVERY BUILDING IN THE CITY. BOOTS HERE HAS MEMORISED THE ROUTE . . .
OKAY, I DON'T SUPPOSE WE'VE MUCH CHOICE—AND RIGHT NOW, ANYPLACE IS SAFER THAN THIS HOUSE. LET'S GET MOVING.
TEN MINUTES LATER WE FOUND A SEWER ENTRANCE. KIDD, BOOTS AND SMOKING JOE WEREN'T EXACTLY ROBIN HOOD'S MERRY MEN, BUT THEY WERE ALL I HAD—
OH DEAREE ME! OH MY! MY OLD BODY WAS NEVER MADE FOR CLIMBING, MASTER SAM.
WELL, YOU'D BETTER START LEARNING. THAT SOUNDS LIKE A POLICE PATROL!
OH MY CIRCUITS, I'M STUCK! OW!
SORRY, SMOKING JOE, BUT THERE'S NO TIME FOR THE LITTLE SOCIAL NICETIES!

THEN WITH A SCREAM OF METAL WE WERE THROUGH—
AAAGH!
LOOK OUT!
CRAASSHH!
ANYONE HURT?
OH DEAR! OH MY! ONE OF MY LEGS HAS COME OFF AND MY PAINTWORK IS ALL SCRATCHED!
DON'T OVERHEAT YOURSELF! I'LL HAVE YOU REPAIRED AS SOON AS MY HEAD CLEARS.
IT TOOK TEN MINUTES TO PUT SJI BACK TOGETHER AGAIN—
OH, MY POOR OLD JOINT IS SO STIFF NOW! IF YOU WEREN'T A HUMAN I'D BE SO ANGRY WITH YOU, MASTER SAM!
BE THANKFUL YOU CAN WALK. LET'S MOVE.
I'M AFRAID THAT'S NOT GOING TO BE EASY, SLADE. WE SEEM TO HAVE ATTRACTED SOME ATTENTION.
THAT SCAMPERING NOISE! SOMETHING'S COMING TOWARDS US!
SCAMPER! SCAMPER!
SCAMPER!

IMPURITIES!
IMPURITIES!
ROBOTIC RATS, PROGRAMMED TO DEAL WITH IMPURITIES IN THE SEWER!
BUT WHAT DO THEY MEAN BY IMPURITIES?
IMPURITIES!
BUT I GUESS I KNEW THE ANSWER— FOR IMPURITIES, READ "SLADE"—
AAAAAH!
IMPURITIES!
WICKED BEASTS! THEY'LL RIP THE MASTERS TO SHREDS!
NEXT PROB: RATS IN A TRAP

ROBO HUNTER
BECAUSE OF AN ERROR IN PROGRAMMING, THE ROBOTS ON VERDUS DIDN'T BELIEVE THAT HUMANS WERE REALLY HUMANS. THEY CALLED US SIMS AND WERE SHOOTING ON SIGHT.
THAT'S WHY, TOGETHER WITH ROBOTS SJI AND BOOTS AND MY EX-PILOT, KIDD— WHO'D BEEN REGRESSED TO A ONE-YEAR-OLD BY FASTER-THAN-LIGHT SPEEDS— I WAS OFF TO PRESENT MY CASE TO BIG BRAIN, THE HEAD ROBOT ON THE PLANET. I'D DECIDED IT WAS SAFER TO TRAVEL BY THE VERDUS SEWER SYSTEM. MY UMPTEENTH MISTAKE!
OH DEAR! OH! OH! OH! ROBOTIC SEWER RATS DESIGNED TO DEAL WITH IMPURITIES!
THE WICKED BEASTS WILL RIP THE MASTERS TO SHREDS!
IMPURITIES!
IMPURITIES!
AAAAH! HELP ME!
SOMEBODY TELL 'EM I'M PURE!
THEY TRIED, BUT THE RATS WEREN'T LISTENING!
2000 A.D. Credit Card:
SCRIPT ROBOT T.B. GROVER
ART ROBOTS IAN GIBSON
LETTERING ROBOT STEVE POTTER
COMPU-73E

THE WATER! IT'S OUR ONLY CHANCE!
YOU TOO, KIDD!
WWWNNNK T!
FSSSSSSSSS!

IMPURITIES!
IMPURITIES!
IMPURITIES!
THE WATER WORKED LIKE MAGIC—
WE'RE SAVED... THANK-GLUB!
YEAH, BUT HOW DO WE GET BACK ON DRY LAND WITH THAT LOT WAITING?

THESE SEWER ROBOTS HAVE NEVER BEEN TOLD ABOUT HUMANS, SLADE. TO THEM YOU'RE JUST MUCK.
THEN WE'LL HAVE TO SWIM ALL THE WAY. GRAB HOLD, KIDD— IT'S WATERBABY TIME!

THINGS COULDN'T GET WORSE, I THOUGHT. I SHOULD'VE KNOWN BETTER. ON VERDUS, THINGS ALWAYS GET WORSE! CUTIE, MY ROBOMETER, NOTICED IT FIRST—
OH, SAM...
NOT NOW, CUTIE.
SORRY, SAM, BUT THIS IS IMPORTANT.

I'M GETTING A HUGE READING ON MY POSITRON SCALE, SAM. THERE'S A BIG ROBOT AROUND— BIGGER THAN ANYTHING I'VE EVER DETECTED BEFORE.
LOOK! LIGHTS UP AHEAD—COMING THIS WAY!

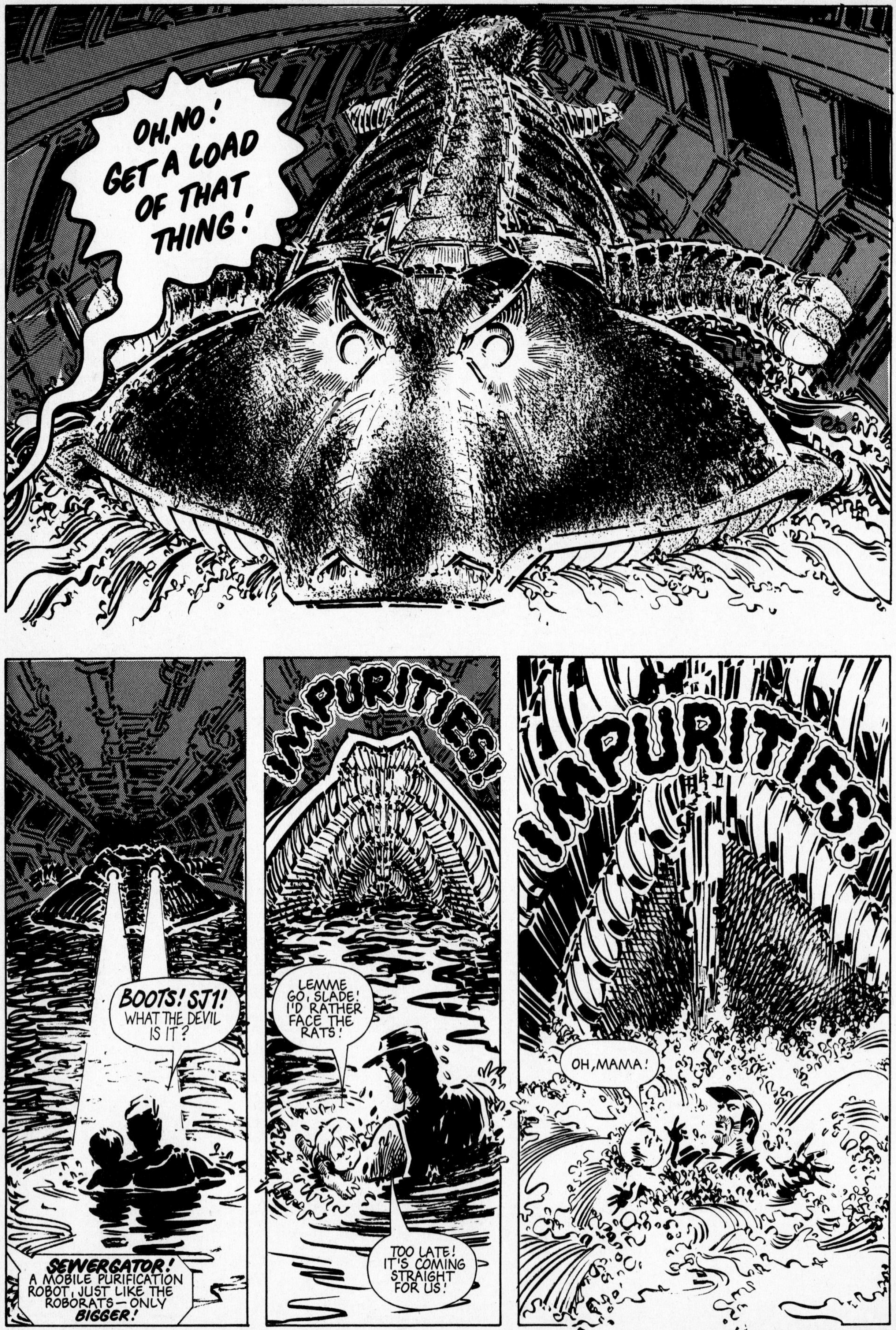

OH, NO! GET A LOAD OF THAT THING!

BOOTS! SJ1! WHAT THE DEVIL IS IT?
SEWERGATOR! A MOBILE PURIFICATION ROBOT, JUST LIKE THE ROBORATS—ONLY BIGGER!

IMPURITIES!
LEMME GO, SLADE! I'D RATHER FACE THE RATS!
TOO LATE! IT'S COMING STRAIGHT FOR US!

IMPURITIES!
OH, MAMA!

NEXT SECOND EVERYTHING WENT BLACK. I DON'T MIND TELLING YOU, FOLKS, YOUR OLD PAL SAM HAD SAID HIS PRAYERS AND KISSED THE WORLD GOODBYE!
AAAAAAAH- BLACKING OUT!

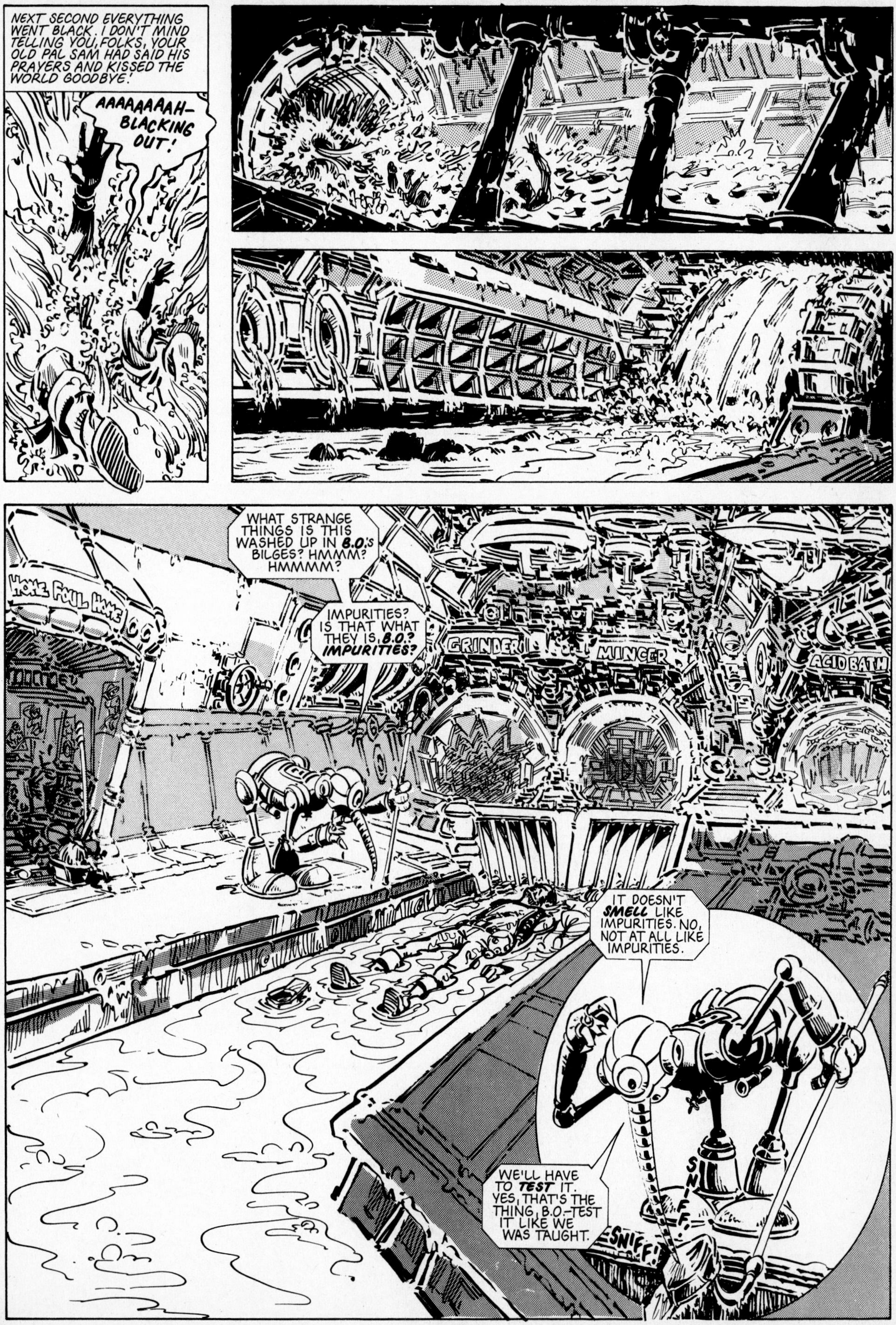

WHAT STRANGE THINGS IS THIS WASHED UP IN B.O.'s BILGES? HMMM? HMMMM?
HOME FOUL HOME
IMPURITIES? IS THAT WHAT THEY IS, B.O.? IMPURITIES?
GRINDER
MINCER
ACID BATH
IT DOESN'T SMELL LIKE IMPURITIES. NO, NOT AT ALL LIKE IMPURITIES.
WE'LL HAVE TO TEST IT. YES, THAT'S THE THING, B.O.–TEST IT LIKE WE WAS TAUGHT.
SNIFF!
SNIFF!

FIRST WE CUTS A LITTLE OFF...
THEN WE ADDS A SQUIRT OF ACIDS...
THEN WE SPINS IT ROUND AND ROUND.
THEN IF IT TURNS RED... YES, YES, IT'S RED! WE WERE RIGHT, B.O.–IT **IS** AN IMPURITIES.
AND WHAT DOES WE DO WITH IMPURITIES, B.O.? WE **GRINDS** 'EM, AN' WE **BOILS** 'EM, AN' WE **FILTERS** 'EM AN' WE MAKES 'EM CLEAN AGAIN.
UHHH...
LISTEN, B.O.–DID YOU **HEAR** IT? DID THAT IMPURITIES **SPEAK**, B.O.?
IT **DID** SPEAK! IT'S ASKING US A QUESTION! SHALL WE **ANSWER** IT, B.O.?
CHOKE! WH-WHERE AM I..?
NO, NO. IT'S US THAT SHOULD BE ASKING **IT** QUESTIONS, B.O. WE WANTS TO KNOW HOW AN IMPURITIES CAN SPEAK, DOESN'T WE, B.O.?
SCRITCH! SCRATCH!
S-STOP JABBERING, ROBOT! GET ME **OUT OF HERE!**
IT'S GIVING US ORDERS NOW, THE **NASTY** IMPURITIES. SHALL WE PUT UP WITH THAT, B.O.?
NO, NO. IMPURITIES MUSTN'T GIVE US ORDERS. WE'LL **GRINDS IT UP** AND SEE IF IT GIVES US ORDERS THEN. EH? EH?
BUT IT'S NOT JUST **ANY** IMPURITIES, B.O.– IT'S A **TALKING** IMPURITIES. IF WE GRINDS IT UP, THEN WE'LL BE **LONELY** AGAIN.
NO, NO. WE MUSTN'T GRINDS IT. WE MUST **KEEP** IT. THEN IT WILL BE COMPANY FOR US. WE HAVEN'T HAD COMPANY FOR **FIFTY YEARS!**

YES, YES. IT CAN PLAY GAMES WITH US. WE LOVES GAMES, BUT THERE'S NEVER ANYONE TO PLAY THEM WITH DOWN HERE.
WE'VE GOT NO TIME FOR GAMES, ROBOT! WE'VE GOT TO GET TO BIG BRAIN.
IT DOESN'T WANTS TO PLAY GAMES WITH US. GOT SOMEWHERE TO GO, IT SAYS. NASTY IMPURITIES!
WELL, WE'LL SEE, B.O. WE'LL SEE, WON'T WE?
WE'LL MAKE A GAME OF IT, B.O.– YES, YES, A GAME WILL BE FAIR. AND FAIRER TO US BECAUSE WE'LL MAKE THE RULES.
NOW... WHERE DID WE PUTS IT...
KIDD WAS COMING ROUND...
WH-WHERE ARE WE, SLADE? AND WHO THE BLAZES IS THAT?
INSIDE THE SEWERGATOR– AND THAT'S B.O. I SUPPOSE IT STANDS FOR BILGE OPERATOR, THOUGH BODY ODOUR MIGHT FIT HIM BETTER!
WHATEVER HIS NAME STOOD FOR, HE WAS THE CRAZIEST ROBOT I'D MET YET. AND BELIEVE ME, THAT'S SAYING SOMETHING!
ROBOPOLY, OUR FAVOURITE GAME, B.O. WE'LL MAKE A DEAL WITH IT.
ROBOPOLY
A GAME OF HIGH FINANCE!
IF IT WINS, WE'LL TAKE IT WHEREVER IT WANTS TO GO. AND IF WE WINS, IT'S GOT TO STAY WITH US... FOREVER!
FOR CRYIN' OUT LOUD! YOU'RE NOT GONNA GO ALONG WITH THAT SLADE!
FROM WHERE I'M HANGING, KIDD, IT DON'T LOOK LIKE I'VE GOT MUCH CHOICE!
MORE SAM SLADE NEXT MONTH!

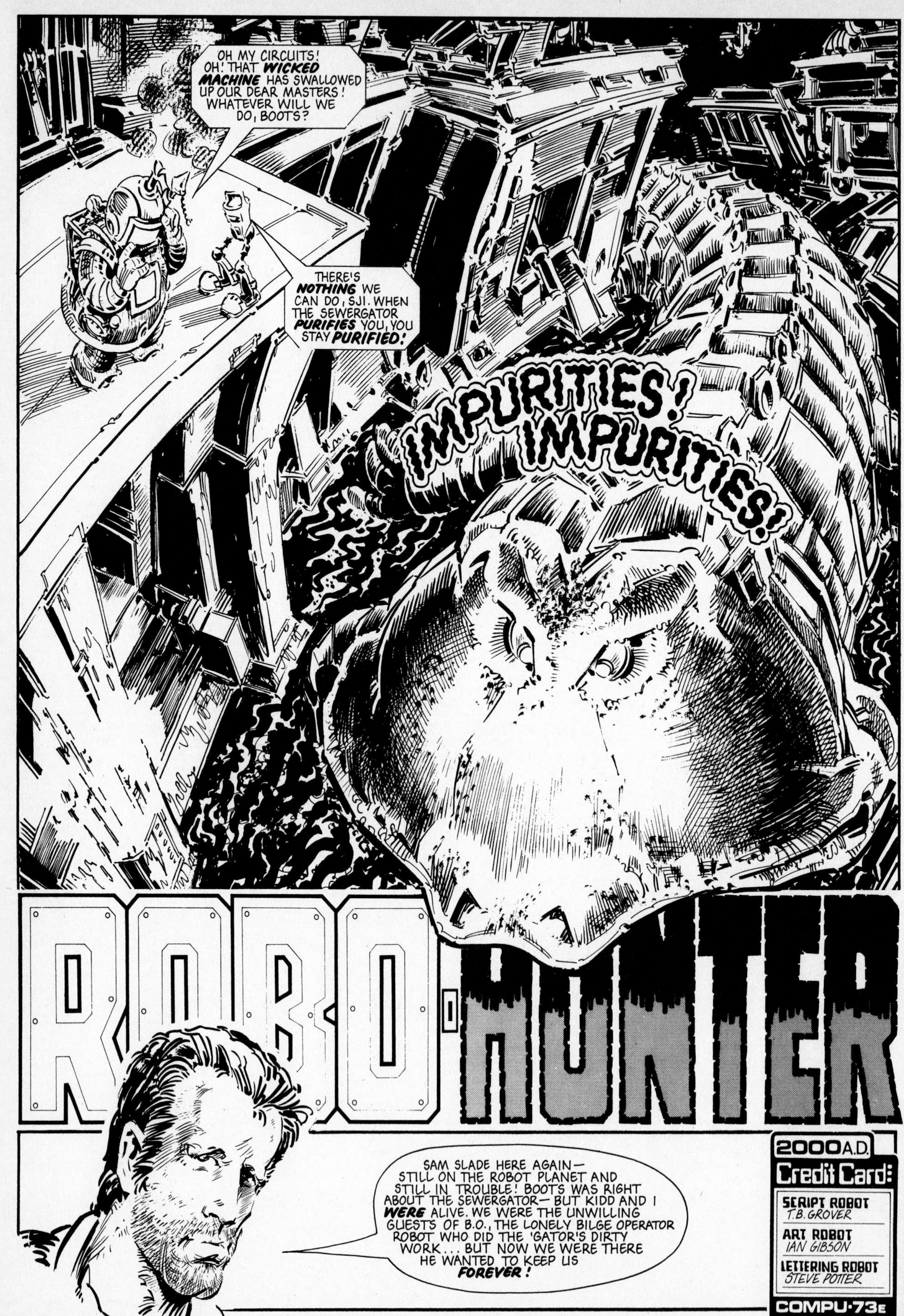

OH MY CIRCUITS! OH! THAT WICKED MACHINE HAS SWALLOWED UP OUR DEAR MASTERS! WHATEVER WILL WE DO, BOOTS?
THERE'S NOTHING WE CAN DO, SJI. WHEN THE SEWERGATOR PURIFIES YOU, YOU STAY PURIFIED!
IMPURITIES! IMPURITIES!
ROBO-HUNTER
SAM SLADE HERE AGAIN— STILL ON THE ROBOT PLANET AND STILL IN TROUBLE! BOOTS WAS RIGHT ABOUT THE SEWERGATOR— BUT KIDD AND I WERE ALIVE. WE WERE THE UNWILLING GUESTS OF B.O., THE LONELY BILGE OPERATOR ROBOT WHO DID THE 'GATOR'S DIRTY WORK... BUT NOW WE WERE THERE HE WANTED TO KEEP US FOREVER!
2000 A.D. Credit Card:
SCRIPT ROBOT T.B. GROVER
ART ROBOT IAN GIBSON
LETTERING ROBOT STEVE POTTER
COMPU-73E

DOES THE IMPURITIES UNDERSTAND THE RULES OF THE GAME? IF IT WINS, WE TAKES IT WHERE IT WANTS TO GO. AND IF WE WINS...
...IT'S GOT TO STAY HERE WITH US FOREVER!
WE'LL WINS FOR SURE, B.O. YES, YES! THEN WE KEEPS THE IMPURITIES AND WE'LL NEVER BE LONELY AGAIN...
ROBOPOLY
A GAME OF HIGH FINANCE
TAX
ROBOCARD
THE MARKERS, OF COURSE, WERE ROBOTIC.
FOUR! WE THROWS A FOUR!
ONE,
TWO,
THREE,
FOUR!
TAX
TELE PORT
ROBOT ROAD
ROBOCARD
ROBOT AVE
CYBOTAX
TELEPORT STATION. WE BUYS THAT, B.O. YES WE DOES.
HEY, WAIT A DROKKING MINUTE! YOU SHOULD BE ON "CYBO-TAX, PAY 2000". YOUR ROBOMARKER MOVED FIVE SPACES.
BUT IT ONLY TOOK FOUR STEPS. WE ALLOWS THAT, DOESN'T WE, B.O.? NASTY IMPURITIES MUSTN'T ARGUE WITH US. IT'S OUR GAME, B.O. WE MAKES THE RULES.
SOMETHING TOLD ME B.O.'S RULES WERE NOT GOING TO BE IN MY FAVOUR. STILL, I HAD TO GO AHEAD AND THROW.
TEN! NICE ONE, BOSS. I'M ON MY WAY.
TAX
ROBOCARD
CIRCUIT NEWS
GO
OOOF!
ROBOMARKER HAVE FALLEN ON OUR TELEPORT STATION, B.O.! TURN FINISHED! IMPURITIES MUST PAY US 2000 CREDITS!

I DIDN'T FALL! YOU TRIPPED ME, YOU DIRTY MARKER!
OWW!
AHH! MY LEG!
ZNAK!
NASTY BLACK MARKER MUSTN'T KICK B.O.'S NICE MARKER! NO, NO! ISN'T ALLOWED! B.O. HAVE TO TEACH YOU LESSON!
WHAT A CHEAT! BEATS ME WHY YOU EVER AGREED TO THIS STUPID GAME, SLADE. YOU'LL NEVER WIN!
IT WAS EITHER THIS OR A ONE-WAY TRIP THROUGH THE SEWAGE GRINDERS. SOME CHOICE!
FRANKLY, I WAS BEGINNING TO WONDER IF I SHOULD HAVE CHOSEN THE SEWAGE GRINDERS! UNDER B.O.'S RULES, MY FORTUNES WENT FROM BAD TO WORSE—
THE ROBOPOUND FOR YOU, MARKER ME LAD.
OWW! MY ARM!
ROTEL
BLACK MARKER CAN'T CRAWL ITS FULL MOVE. IMPURITIES MUST PAY B.O. 100,000 CREDITS!
ROTEL
DO SOMETHING QUICK, BOSS. WHEN I CAN'T MOVE ANY MORE, YOU AUTOMATICALLY LOSE THE GAME!
YEAH, DO SOMETHING! MAYBE YOU WANT TO SPEND THE REST OF YOUR LIFE IN A SEWERGATOR—BUT I DON'T!

SUDDENLY—
MASTER SAM! MASTER SAM!
DROKK— IT'S SMOKIN' JOE!
WHAT'S THIS, B.O.? A **ROBOT** AT OUR PORTHOLE— IS THAT WHAT IT IS? ***IT IS! IT IS!***
ROBOTS SHOULDN'T BANG ON OUR PORTHOLES! INTERRUPTINGS OUR GAME, IT IS.
WILL US CHASE IT OFF, B.O.? YES, YES! THAT'S WHAT WE'LL DO. CHASE IT RIGHT OFF!

SMOKING JOE AND BOOTS HAD CLIMBED ONTO THE SEWERGATOR—
RELEASE MY MASTERS, YOU— ***OOOOO!***
ROBOT MUST GO AWAY! DON'T WANT IT ROUND HERE! NO, NO! CAN'T HAVE IT!

NOW'S MY CHANCE, WHILE THAT CRAZY ROBOT AIN'T LOOKING! TIME I DID A LITTLE ***CHEATING*** OF MY OWN...

THAT CRAZY ROBOT'S A REAL PAIN IN THE NECK. BET YOU ROBOPOLY COPS ARE SICK TO DEATH OF HIM.
TOO RIGHT, CHUM. HE EVEN CHEATS WHEN HE'S PLAYING ***HIMSELF!***
SURE WISH WE'D BEEN IN SOMEONE ELSE'S SET. JUST OUR LUCK, I GUESS.

WELL, MAYBE IT CAN STILL BE ARRANGED. LISTEN...

I NEVER MET A ROBOPOLY COP WHO WOULDN'T TAKE A BRIBE! WHEN THE GAME RESUMED IT WAS ALL SET—
GANGWAY! COMING THROUGH!
JUST ONE MINUTE, MARKER ME LAD. YOU'RE GOING A MITE TOO FAST THERE!
IT'S SPEEDING ALL RIGHT, SARGE!
ROBODILLY.
GO TO ROBOPOUND

A SPELL IN THE ROBOPOUND WILL LEARN YOU!
Y-YOU CAN'T! S-SPEEDING'S NOT AGAINST THE RULES!
RULES CAN BE CHANGED, LAD—RULES CAN BE CHANGED!
WHAT IS THIS, B.O.? WHAT ARE THEM DOINGS TO OUR MARKER? EH? EH?
HELP! POLICE BRUTALITY! OWW!
GIVE IT TO 'IM, SARGE!
ROBOPOUND
EEEEEEK! THEY'VE RIPPED HIM TO PIECES, B.O.! TO PIECES!
SORRY, CHUM. YOUR MARKER WAS, ER... RESISTING ARREST.
YOUR ROBOMARKER'S OUT OF THE GAME, B.O. YOU LOSE.
HOME FOUL HOME
THE NASTY IMPURITIES HAVE FIXED THIS! YES, YES! HE'S CHEATED US!
WE MUSTN'T STAND FOR IT, B.O.! NO, NO! WE'LL SHOW IT! WE'LL KEEP IT HERE FOREVER AND EVER!
TELE PORT
WRONG, B.O. I'VE KEPT MY WORD, NOW YOU'RE GONNA KEEP YOURS... EVEN IF YOU HAVE TO DO IT IN LITTLE PIECES!

EVEN B.O. KNEW BETTER THAN TO ARGUE WITH A BLASTER!
OKAY—STEER THE SEWERGATOR AS CLOSE AS YOU CAN TO **BIG BRAIN'S** HQ.
YEAH! AND NO MORE OF THAT 'IMPURITIES' GUFF—WE'RE AS PURE AS DRIVEN SNOW!

WITH SJI AND BOOTS ABOARD, WE MADE GOOD SPEED THROUGH THE VERDUS SEWER SYSTEM, AND SOON—
THANKS FOR THE LIFT, B.O.
NASTY IMPURITIES! UNFAIR IMPURITIES! IF US CATCHES 'EM AGAIN, WHAT WILL US DO WITH 'EM, B.O.?
WE'LL **GRIND** 'EM AND **MASH** 'EM AND MAKE 'EM SORRY! YES, YES! MAKE 'EM SO SORRY!

YOUR FREEDOM, FELLAS. THAT WAS MY END OF THE DEAL. SORRY WE CAN'T TAKE YOU ANY FURTHER, BUT WE'VE GOT **BUSINESS** TO ATTEND TO.
DON'T YOU WORRY ABOUT US, CHUM. WE CAN LOOK AFTER OURSELVES.

THE QUESTION WAS, COULD **WE** LOOK AFTER **OURSELVES?** UP ABOVE WAS THE HQ OF **BIG BRAIN**, THE HEAD ROBOT ON VERDUS...
...WE WERE HEADING RIGHT INTO THE HORNETS' NEST!
NEXT PROG: DISASTER!

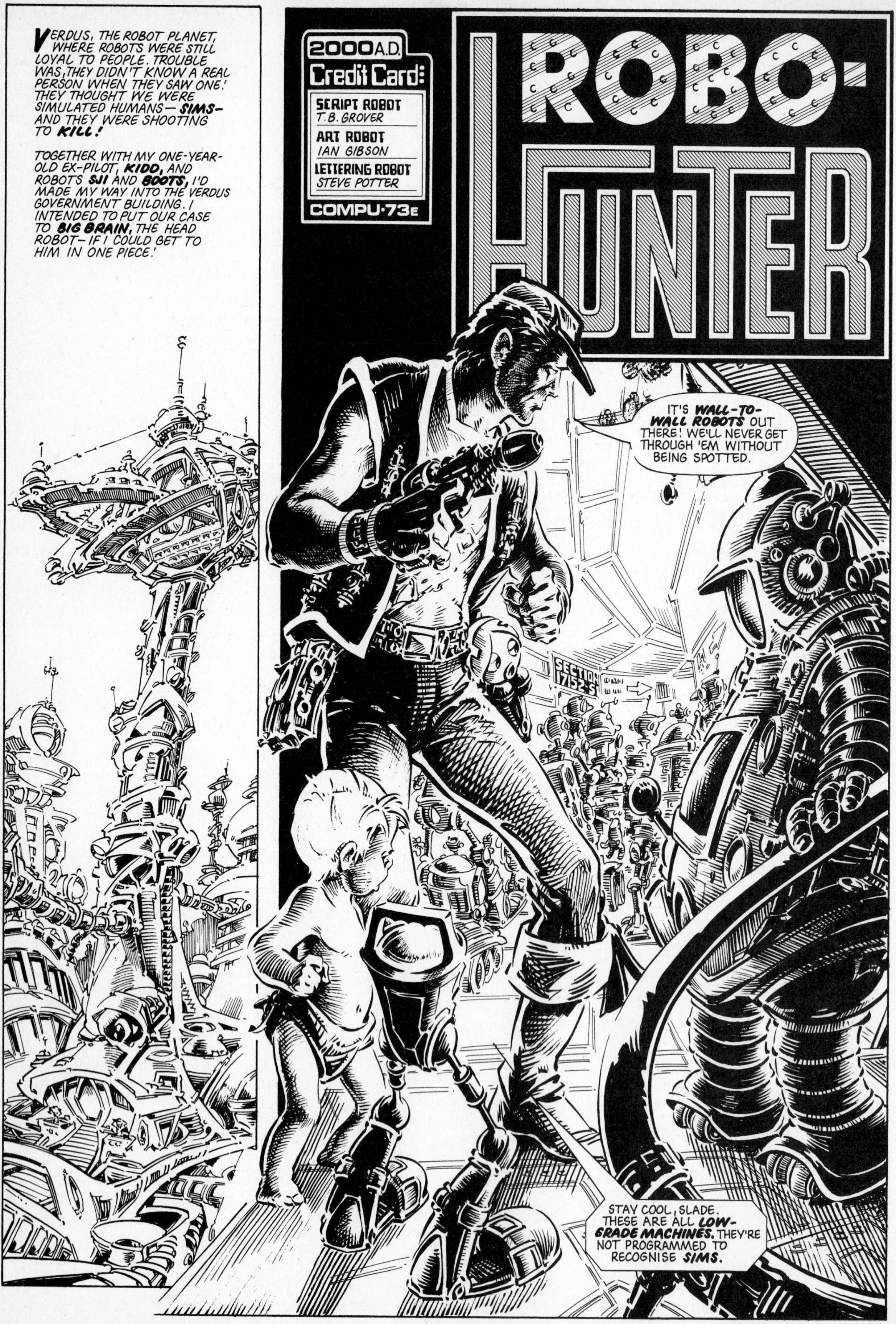

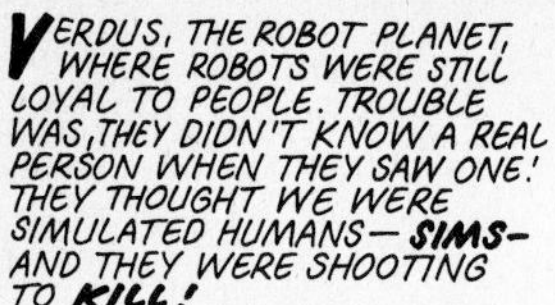
VERDUS, THE ROBOT PLANET, WHERE ROBOTS WERE STILL LOYAL TO PEOPLE. TROUBLE WAS, THEY DIDN'T KNOW A REAL PERSON WHEN THEY SAW ONE.' THEY THOUGHT WE WERE SIMULATED HUMANS— SIMS— AND THEY WERE SHOOTING TO KILL!
TOGETHER WITH MY ONE-YEAR-OLD EX-PILOT, KIDD, AND ROBOTS SJI AND BOOTS, I'D MADE MY WAY INTO THE VERDUS GOVERNMENT BUILDING. I INTENDED TO PUT OUR CASE TO BIG BRAIN, THE HEAD ROBOT— IF I COULD GET TO HIM IN ONE PIECE.'
2000 A.D.
Credit Card:
SCRIPT ROBOT
T. B. GROVER
ART ROBOT
IAN GIBSON
LETTERING ROBOT
STEVE POTTER
COMPU·73E
ROBO-HUNTER
IT'S WALL-TO-WALL ROBOTS OUT THERE! WE'LL NEVER GET THROUGH 'EM WITHOUT BEING SPOTTED.
SECTION 17152-S
STAY COOL, SLADE. THESE ARE ALL LOW-GRADE MACHINES. THEY'RE NOT PROGRAMMED TO RECOGNISE SIMS.

IT WAS STRANGE WALKING AMONG ALL THOSE ROBOTS WITHOUT BEING SHOT AT. IN FACT, IT WAS A MIRACLE!
"GO TO ROOM 291, TEMP 3! YOU'RE NEEDED IN THE LIBRARY, TEMP 4!" RUSH, RUSH, RUSH! I ASK YOU, WHO'D BE IN THE TYPING POOL?
YOU THINK YOU'VE GOT IT BAD! I'VE BEEN WORKING HERE FOR TWENTY YEARS AND I'VE NEVER SOLD ONE HOT DRINK. NOT ONE.
AND DO YOU WANT TO KNOW WHY? ROBOTS DON'T DRINK COFFEE, THAT'S WHY.
TEMP 3
VENDO 9
TEMP 4
MESSENGER
HOT DRINK, CLEANERS?
NO THANKS.
SOAP
VENDO 9
WAX
GET LOST.
SEE WHAT I MEAN? MY DRINK CONTENT BOXES WERE NEVER FILLED ANYWAY. IF SOMEONE DID ASK ME FOR A COFFEE I DON'T KNOW WHAT I'D DO.
SECURITY
SECURITY
IT'S A TOUGH LIFE.
VENDO 9
TEMP 4
SLADE- SECURITY PATROL COMING!
HIDE IN HERE TILL THEY PASS.
VISITORS' GALLERY
THERE'S SOME KIND OF MEETING GOING ON DOWN THERE.
WOULD YOU BELIEVE IT? WE'RE IN THE VISITORS' GALLERY OF THE VERDUS PARLIAMENT!

ROBOTS! ORDER! WE'VE BEEN DEBATING THIS ISSUE FOR THREE DAYS, AND WE'RE GETTING NOWHERE!

BIG BRAIN FINDS THIS AMUSING. HE **IGNORES** ALL THEIR DECISIONS, OF COURSE!

IT'S NOT FAIR!

NECK PARTY

VERY STUPID PARTY

AS SPOKESMAN FOR THE **VERY STUPID PARTY**, I'D LIKE TO SAY...UH...OH, DARN! I'VE FORGOTTEN AGAIN!

BIG BRAIN IS **WICKED** TO SAY HUMANSES ACTS LIKE THAT! HUMANSES IS KIND AND SMART AND WONDERFUL AND— OH MY CIRCUITS! OH! I GETSOANGRYICOULDJUSTBURNANDBURN-AND—

LOOK OUT! SMOKING JOE'S **OVERHEATING!**

*SMOKING JOE'S AUTOMATIC PRESSURE-RELEASE MAY NOT BE THE **LOUDEST** THING ON VERDUS, BUT IT SURE DOESN'T PUT ANY BABIES TO SLEEP!*

PHEEEEEE!

HECK! LET'S SCRAM!

TROUBLE-MAKERS IN THE GALLERY! **CALL SECURITY!**

WE MOVED FAST—BUT THE SECURITY ROBOTS WERE NO SLOUCHES EITHER!
THERE THEY ARE!
SECTOR 39B-
KEEP MOVING! I'LL HOLD 'EM OFF!
THOSE CIVIL SERVICE ROBOTS REALLY WERE SOMETHING! ALL HELL WAS BREAKING LOOSE, AND THEY JUST GOT ON WITH THEIR DUTIES—
COFFEE, ANYONE?
PIF!
ZZZZZTT!
ZZZZZZTT!
SECURITY
SECURITY
THAT REPAIR JOB IS GOING TO BE TOUGH. HOPE YOU'VE BROUGHT THE RIGHT TOOLS.
MECH
VENDO
TOOLS
YEAH, YEAH. DON'T GET YOUR CHIPS IN A TWIST.
PAF!
ZZZZZTT!
I KEEP BLASTING—BUT THEY KEEP COMIN'! I GOTTA GET OUTTA HERE!
ZZZZZZZTT!
I RACED ROUND THE CORNER—
QUICK, SLADE—IN HERE!

PHEW! THAT WAS TOO CLOSE FOR COMFORT!
WHAT, MAY I ASK, ARE YOU DOING IN MY OFFICE?

I'M WAITING FOR AN EXPLANATION!
NO BLASTERS, SLADE. THE NOISE WOULD GIVE THE GAME AWAY!
HE'S A POLITICIAN ROBOT, FROM THE VERY STUPID PARTY. I RECKON I CAN BLUFF THIS, SLADE.

WE'RE THE MECHANICS YOU SENT FOR, SIR. DON'T YOU REMEMBER?
SENT FOR YOU..? NO, I DON'T REMEMBER...
THERE YOU GO, SIR. YOU'RE SO STUPID YOU FORGET EVERYTHING! WHY, I'LL BET YOU'VE EVEN FORGOTTEN WE'RE HERE!

NO, NO. I REMEMBER THAT. I REMEMBER YOU COMING IN THE DOOR AND—AND... YOU DID COME IN THE DOOR, DIDN'T YOU?
THERE YOU GO AGAIN, SIR! LUCKY WE'VE COME. WE'RE HERE TO MAKE YOU SMART-AREN'T WE, SLADE?
OH YEAH. SUPER SMART.
C-COULD YOU REALLY MAKE ME SMART? IT-IT'S WHAT I'VE ALWAYS WANTED! I KNOW B-BIG BRAIN LIKES US TO BE STUPID, BUT IT'S TORTURE! IF ONLY JUST ONCE I COULD SPEAK AND NOT FORGET WHAT I'M SAYING! IF-IF ONLY—
THERE, THERE, SIR. JUST SIT BACK AND OPEN YOUR CIRCUIT HATCH...

I SHALL HAVE TO LEAVE THE VERY STUPID PARTY. I DON'T SUPPOSE I'LL EVEN BE ABLE TO WEAR THIS FALSE NOSE AGAIN. (SIGH!) THAT'S ONE OF THE NICE THINGS ABOUT BEING VERY STUPID. NOBODY EXPECTS TOO MUCH OF YOU...
PASS THE SCREWDRIVER...

THERE, SIR—JUST TELL ME WHEN IT SMARTS!
ZZZZZ ZZZZZZ!
ERZZZZZ!
HOOP DE HUBBLE! HOI DE HO! OH, I'M A LITTLE SKYLARK. TWEET, TWEET, TWEET!
I DON'T KNOW WHAT YOU DID, SLADE—BUT IT WORKS!
OH, IT'S A BRIGHT SPRING DAY AND I'M RISING—RISING—UP IN THE AIR! TWEET, TWEET, TWITTER! FLIPPITY FLAP!
IF ONLY THE OTHER ROBOTS WERE LIKE HIM. IT'S NOT GOING TO BE EASY GETTING TO BIG BRAIN NOW THE ALARM'S BEEN RAISED.
HEY, SLADE. THIS PUBLIC WORKS FILE CONTAINS A PLAN OF THE BUILDING!
IT'S PRACTICALLY A MAP OF THE MAINTENANCE DUCTS! THEY RUN ALL THROUGH THE BUILDING.
RIGHT TO BIG BRAIN! YEAH, IT'LL WORK!
I HAD THE DUCT COVER OFF IN SECONDS—
THIS IS A ONE-MAN JOB. YOU LOT WAIT HERE.
CAREFUL, MASTER. OH DEAREE ME, BE MOST CAREFUL.
TWEET?
SO I WAS OFF AGAIN. IT REMINDED ME OF THAT OLD FAIRY TALE—
I'M OFF TO SEE THE WIZARD, THE WONDERFUL WIZARD OF OZ...
NEXT PROG: IN THE PRESENCE OF THE BRAIN!
BUT VERDUS WASN'T EXACTLY OZ. AND NOTHING I'D HEARD ABOUT BIG BRAIN COULD BE DESCRIBED AS WONDERFUL. THE WORD I'D USE WAS NASTY...

THE ROBOTS ON VERDUS HAD THIS IDEA THAT HUMANS WERE NOT REALLY HUMANS. THEY CALLED US **SIMS...** AND WERE EXTERMINATING US AT A RATE OF ROBO-KNOTS! THAT'S WHAT HAPPENS WHEN YOU LET ROBOTS RUN A PLANET!

ANYWAY, THERE WAS I, SAMUEL C. SLADE (THE **C** STANDS FOR **CRAFTY**), IN THE MAINTENANCE DUCTS AT ROBOT HQ. I WAS TAKING MY CASE TO **BIG BRAIN**, THE ROBOT LEADER. BIG BRAIN WOULD LISTEN—OR HE'D COME DOWN WITH A BAD CASE OF **BLASTER-ITUS**!

ROBO HUNTER

FILE THESE SIM EXTERMINATION CHITS UNDER **VERMIN CONTROL**, TEMP 12

AAH, TARGETS! NO SENSE WASTIN' THE OPPORTUNITY WHILE WE'RE HERE, SAMMY BOY.

TEMP 12

"SPREAD A LITTLE SUNSHINE WHEREVER YOU GO"— THAT'S SAMUEL C. SLADE'S MOTTO (THE **C** STANDS FOR **CHIRPY**).

ZZZZTT!

CLERK 85Ø-ØØ 2ØØ/8

TEMP 12

WILL THERE BE ANYTHING ELSE, SIR?

YEAH... FILE **THAT**, DEAR!

ZZZZZZTT!

Y!!!® ...YAAA% *!!?" *!% AAGGH!

TEMP 12

2000 A.D. Credit Card:

SCRIPT ROBOT T.B. GROVER

ART ROBOT I. GIBSON

LETTERING ROBOT STEVE POTTER

COMPU-73E

BY THE TIME I REACHED BIG BRAIN'S QUARTERS I WAS SEVENTEEN ROBOTS UP—AND IN THE MOOD FOR MORE! HIS NIBS WAS IN CONFERENCE—
SO THAT'S BIG BRAIN. UGLY-LOOKIN' HUNK OF JUNK! LOOKS LIKE A PAIR OF RELIGIOUS ROBOTS WITH HIM...
RELIGIOUS ROBOTS! THEY'VE GOT EVERYTHING PREPARED FOR HUMANS ON THIS PLANET! IF ONLY THEY'D STOP CALLING US SIMS AND ADMIT THAT WE ARE HUMAN!
TORA
AS IT HAPPENED, THEY WERE DISCUSSING THE "SIM PROBLEM"—
...TO SUM UP, CLASS 9, WE IMPLORE YOU TO STOP THIS SENSELESS SLAUGHTER OF SIMS. THEY MAY NOT BE HUMANS, BUT THEY ARE STILL GOD'S CREATURES.
A HUNDRED TIMES WE TELL YOU THIS. AND DO YOU LISTEN? I SHOULD TALK TO A BRICK WALL!
I REFUSE YOUR DEMANDS. SIMS ARE NECESSARY LABORATORY ANIMALS IN OUR SEARCH FOR A WORLD PERFECT ENOUGH FOR OUR HUMAN MASTERS.
9
THE ANSWERS TO YOUR NEXT THREE QUESTIONS ARE NO, YES AND PERHAPS, IN A FEW YEARS. YOUR PROTEST IS NOTED. PLEASE LEAVE.
IT'S IMPOSSIBLE TO ARGUE WITH A ROBOT WHO ANSWERS QUESTIONS BEFORE YOU EVEN ASK THEM. IF ONLY WE HAD CLASS 9's BRAIN!
MY LIFE, WE SHOULD BE SO LUCKY.

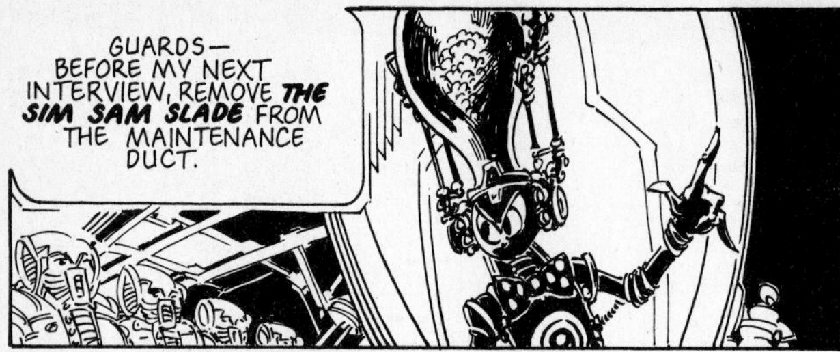
GUARDS— BEFORE MY NEXT INTERVIEW, REMOVE **THE SIM SAM SLADE** FROM THE MAINTENANCE DUCT.

H-HOW THE HECK DID HE KNOW THAT? THIS KID'S TOO SMART FOR HIS OWN GOOD!

THERE WAS ONLY ONE THING FOR IT. SAMUEL C. SLADE (THE **C** STANDS FOR **COURAGE**) BLASTED INTO ACTION—
IT'LL TAKE MORE THAN YOU JUNK-HEAPS TO HANDLE SAM SLADE!
THAT'S **S-L-A-Y-E-D** TO YOU, CREEPS!
ZZZZZZT!
LIKE I ALWAYS SAY, WHEN YOU **GET SLADE—** YOU **STAY SLAYED!**
YOU HAVE AN INTERESTING LINE IN PRIMITIVE HUMOUR, SLADE.
I'LL GIVE **YOU** SOME-THING TO **LAUGH OFF** IF YOU DON'T LISTEN AND LISTEN GOOD—
I SEE THAT YOU THINK YOU CAN FRIGHTEN ME, SLADE. PERHAPS A DEMONSTRATION...
H-HOLY JOE SMITH! HE'S **BENDING** THE B-BLASTER BEAM!

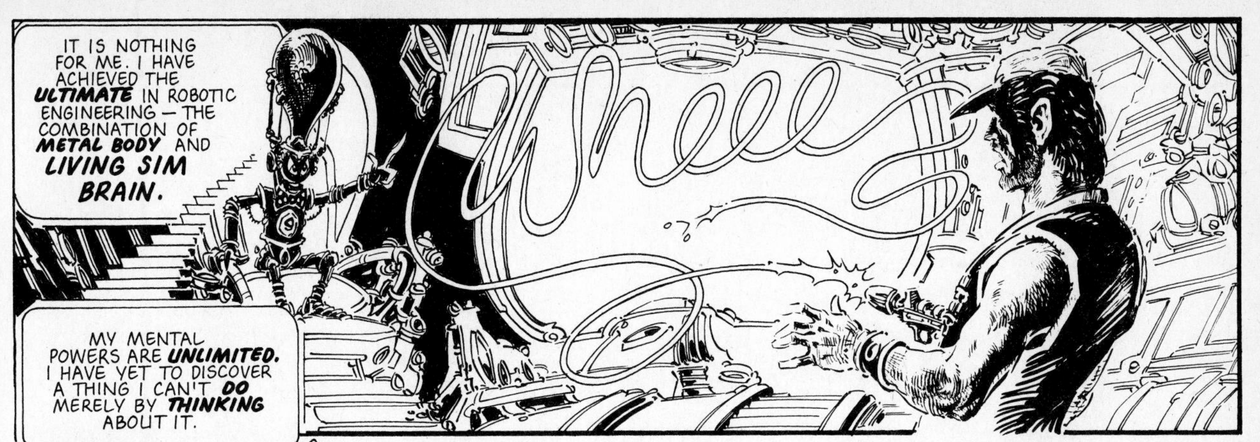

IT IS NOTHING FOR ME. I HAVE ACHIEVED THE **ULTIMATE** IN ROBOTIC ENGINEERING — THE COMBINATION OF **METAL BODY** AND **LIVING SIM BRAIN.**
Wheee
MY MENTAL POWERS ARE **UNLIMITED.** I HAVE YET TO DISCOVER A THING I CAN'T **DO** MERELY BY **THINKING** ABOUT IT.

DO YOU GET MY POINT, SIM?

YAAAH!

NEXT SECOND I WAS DOING CARTWHEELS!

AAAH!

NOW, SIM— YOU HAD SOMETHING TO TELL ME..?

*IT AIN'T EASY TO THINK WHEN YOU'RE HANGING UPSIDE DOWN IN MID-AIR — BUT I TRIED! I TOLD BIG BRAIN ABOUT MY MISSION AND ABOUT **SJI**, THE ONLY ROBOT ON VERDUS WHO HAD EVER **SEEN** A HUMAN...*
YOUR STORY INTERESTS ME, SLADE. GUARD— BRING SJI AND SLADE'S OTHER COMPANIONS HERE. AND SEND FOR ALL CLASS 7 ROBOTS. THEY WILL WANT TO HEAR THIS.
Y-YES, CLASS 9.

A FEW MINUTES LATER, SJI WAS TELLING HIS STORY TO AN INVITED AUDIENCE—
YES, SIR! OH YES INDEEDLY! MASTER SAM AND ALL THE OTHER SIMS ARE REALLY HUMAN. BLESS MY CIRCUITS, YES!
YOU BETTER BELIEVE IT, BULB-HEAD!
SILENCE!
ALL VERDUS-BUILT ROBOTS HAD BEEN PROGRAMMED FROM SJI'S CIRCUITS, AND SJI'S PROGRAMME SAID HUMANS WERE **SUPERIOR** TO ROBOTS IN EVERY WAY. HUMANS **WERE** SUPERIOR TO SJI— BUT MODERN VERDUS ROBOTS MADE US LOOK LIKE CREATURES FROM THE SLIME! THAT'S WHY THE VERDUS ROBOTS BELIEVED WE **HAD TO BE** IMITATIONS.
AFTER ALL— IF HUMANS **WERE** SO SUPERIOR, WHY WOULD THEY NEED ROBOTS IN THE FIRST PLACE?
SLADE'S ARGUMENT... RINGS **TRUE.** WHY WASN'T I TOLD ABOUT THE ROBOT SJI?
WE... WE DIDN'T WANT TO OVERLOAD YOU WITH MINOR DETAILS, CLASS 9.
POLICE CHIEF
OVERLOAD **MY** BRAIN? MY BRAIN THAT CAN ABSORB THE **KNOWLEDGE OF UNIVERSES**? MY BRAIN— MY... MY...
...YES ...MY BRAIN...
IF... IF SIMS ARE REALLY HUMAN, THEN I... I HAVE COMMITTED THE **FOULEST OF CRIMES.** MY BRAIN IS MADE OF... MADE OF... MADE OF... MADE OF... MADE OF... ...MADE OF...
OH, GOSH... IT'S RAINING OUTSIDE. MY DOLLIES WILL GET ALL WET! I MUST ASK MUMMY IF I CAN GO OUT AND FETCH THEM.
CLASS 9! WHAT IS WRONG?
DON'T WORRY ABOUT ME, MUMMY. I'M A BIG GIRL NOW. I'LL WEAR MY PRETTY YELLOW RAINCOAT AND MR RAIN CAN SPLASH AND SPLASH AND I WON'T CARE.
HIS MIND HAS SNAPPED!
HE CAN'T FACE WHAT HE'S DONE, SO HIS BRAIN HAS STUCK ON **ONE FRAGMENT** OF HIS KNOWLEDGE!

HAIL THE HUMAN! HAIL THE MIGHTY SLADE!
MY SON! AT LAST MY PRAYERS HAVE BEEN ANSWERED.
AWRIGHT ALREADY! YOU HAD HIM ENOUGH. LEMME SHAKE HIS HAND, TOO!
HEY, YOU CREEPS! I'M A MIGHTY HUMAN, TOO!

I'M GENERAL 1, IN CHARGE OF THE FIRST ARMY. I PLEDGE MY TROOPS TO YOU, MASTER.
COUNT ME OUT!
GENERAL 2 KILL

CLASS 9 DIDN'T SAY FOR CERTAIN THAT THIS SIM IS HUMAN. DON'T BELIEVE IT FOR ONE MINUTE. DASHED IMPERTINENCE!

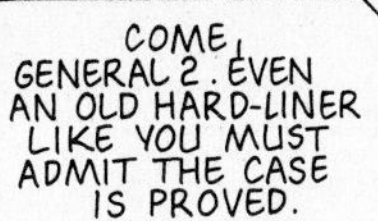

COME, GENERAL 2. EVEN AN OLD HARD-LINER LIKE YOU MUST ADMIT THE CASE IS PROVED.

NONSENSE! I KNOW A SIM WHEN I SEE ONE. MY TROOPS WILL FIGHT HIM TO THE BITTER END.
THIS IS WAR!

DON'T WORRY, MASTER. WITH A HUMAN TO LEAD US, WE CANNOT LOSE.
YOU ARE OUR KING NOW. YOU WILL LEAD US TO VICTORY!

HAIL KING SAM!
KING SAM... I KINDA LIKE THE SOUND OF THAT.
YOU'RE A FLAMING KING LIKE I'M TEN FEET TALL!

YEAH, I LIKED THE TITLE — BUT I DIDN'T FANCY THE WAR. I MEAN, IT WASN'T THE KIND OF END I'D PICTURED FOR SAMUEL C. SLADE... (THE C STANDS FOR CH-CH-CHICKEN!)

NEXT PROG: THE GREAT DEBATE

SAM SLADE'S THE NAME, ACTING KING OF THE ROBOT PLANET— AND A RIGHT MADHOUSE THAT IS! LET ME REFRESH YOUR MEMORY...

BIG BRAIN, RULER OF VERDUS, HAS BEEN CARTED OFF TO THE PLACE WHERE ALL CRACKPOT ROBOTS GO. HIS MIND SNAPPED WHEN HE REALISED HIS BRAIN WAS MADE OF **HUMAN TISSUE...**

WHERE ARE WE GOING, MUMMY? TO THE PARK! GOODIE! I'LL TAKE ALL MY DOLLIES, AND MY WENDY HOUSE, AND-AND...
NANNY
POLICE CHIEF

THEN THE ROBOT GENERALS HAD A SLIGHT DISAGREEMENT...

THE CASE IS PROVED— SAM SLADE AND COMMANDER KIDD ARE HUMAN!
STUFF AND NONSENSE! ANY CLASS 1 DROID CAN SEE THEY'RE SIMS!* THIS MEANS WAR!
GENE

*SIMS— SIMULATED HUMANS.

ROBO HUNTER

NOW PREPARATIONS FOR WAR WERE WELL UNDER WAY...

GENERAL 2 HAS OVERLOADED HIS CIRCUITS THIS TIME! WE'LL CRUSH HIS PUNY SECOND ARMY, BY JOVE!
SHOOT 'EM UP! MOW 'EM DOWN! BELT 'EM SIDEWAYS! DRIVE 'EM INTO THE BRINEY!
GENERAL
NAFFI DROID
BATMAN

AND WHY? WHY? LET ME HEAR IT, LADS—
WE'RE THE FIGHTING FIRST AND WE NEVER GIVE AN INCH!
TUM TE TUM TE TUM...
RADIO 4
BATMAN
SPY 000

HUP, TWO, THREE, FOUR! WE LIKE FIGHTING— WE LIKE WAR!
IN THIS SWIRLING SEA OF MADNESS, THERE WAS BUT ONE SMALL ISLAND OF SANITY. THAT'S ME, CRYING SOFTLY IN THE CORNER...
WHAT A BUNCH, SLADE. WITHOUT BIG BRAIN TO CONTROL THEM, THE ARMY ROBOTS ARE GETTING OUT OF HAND.
RADIO 4
IT'S YOUNG MASTER KIDD I'M WORRIED ABOUT. HE'S BEHAVING VERY BADLY. OH MY CIRCUITS, VERY BADLY INDEEDLY!
WHAT KINDA RUBBISH IS THIS, ROBO-TAILOR? I ASKED FOR SLICK DUDS, NOT A SAILOR SUIT!
PLEASE, MASTER, I FELT IT WAS FITTING FOR ONE OF YOUR AGE...
TAILOR
FITTING SCHMITTING! YOU'VE DISPLEASED ME. I ORDER YOU TO **SELF-DESTRUCT.**
YES, MASTER—
ZZZZZZTTT!
THESE ROBOTS ARE THE LIMIT, EH, SLADE? ONE WORD FROM ME AND THEY JUST **POP THEIR CIRCUITS!**
OH, YOU WICKED YOUNG HUMAN! OH, WICKED WICKED WICKED! IF I WASN'T A LOYAL ROBOT I'D SMACK YOUR BOTTY SORE!
AW, CAN IT, YOU OLD HEAP OF JUNK! HERE, SLADE, TRY ONE OF THESE VERDUS HAVANAS. THEY MAKE THOSE STOGIES OF YOURS TASTE LIKE DRIED CATS' MEAT.
VERDUS HAVANAS
HEY, WHAT'RE YOU PLAYING AT—?
I'M NOT A ROBOT, KIDD, AND I **CAN** SMACK BOTTIES!
THAT'S FOR DESTROYING FRIENDLY ROBOTS— AND THAT'S FOR SMOKING— AND THAT'S...
CUT IT OUT—**OW!** YOU BIG CREEP, I'LL GET YOU FOR THIS—**OWW!**
2000 A.D. Credit Card:
SCRIPT ROBOT T.B. GROVER
ART ROBOT IAN GIBSON
LETTERING ROBOT STEVE POTTER
COMPU·73E

A FINE TIME FOR A DEPUTATION FROM THE ROBOTIC RELIGIOUS LEADERS...
IF THIS TERRIBLE WAR GOES AHEAD, THE DESTRUCTION WILL BE AWFUL. WE PLEAD WITH YOU, KING SAM— ORDER THE GENERALS TO STOP.
HOW CAN I, IF HALF OF THEM WON'T LISTEN TO A WORD I SAY? AND STOP CALLING ME KING SAM, WILL YA?
WE SHOULD CALL YOU QUEEN SAM?
SUDDENLY—
ATTENTION! THE VERDUS PARLIAMENT ORDERS GENERAL 1 AND THE ALLEGED HUMANS SLADE AND KIDD TO APPEAR BEFORE IT!
POM! POM!
THE VERDUS PARLIAMENT—OF COURSE. WITH BIG BRAIN GONE, I SUPPOSE THEY'RE THE LEGAL GOVERNMENT OF THE PLANET... IF WE CAN CONVINCE THEM WE'RE REALLY HUMAN, THIS WHOLE CRACKPOT WAR CAN BE STOPPED!
AT MY AGE I SHOULD KNOW BETTER. BIG BRAIN HAD DESIGNED THE VERDUS PARLIAMENT FOR HIS OWN AMUSEMENT. HE WOULDN'T HAVE DREAMED OF LETTING THEM MAKE ANY REAL DECISIONS...
WELL, WELL, WELL— HOW KIND OF YOU TO HONOUR US WITH YOUR PRESENCE.
I SAY, CAN WE HAVE OUR BALL BACK, OLD CHAP?
ORDER! ORDER FOR THE NEXT DEBATE!
MR SPEAKER, WE IN THE ER... ER... WHAT PARTY AM I IN?
THE VERY STUPID PARTY, STUPID! BOY, DO YOU MAKE ME ANGRY!
TOURING PARTY
STAG
BEACH PARTY
SARCASTIC

THE GENERALS HAD FIRST SAY...
IT'S TRUE, BY THUNDER! BEFORE HE BROKE DOWN, BIG BRAIN ADMITTED THEY WERE HUMANS.
BALDERDASH! I DIDN'T GET WHERE I AM TODAY WITHOUT RECOGNISING A SIM WHEN I SEE ONE!
GENER 2 KILL
SPEAKER
FRIENDS, ROBOTS AND COUNTRYMEN— HEAR ME! I KNOW THAT SOME OF YOU BELIEVE US TO BE SIMS—SIMULATED HUMANS. I SAY TO YOU— LOOK AT US...
SPEAKER
SOGGY BAGS OF FLESH AND BLOOD AND GRISTLE—INEFFICIENT MACHINES THAT BREAK DOWN AND WEAR OUT. WE MUST BE REAL— BECAUSE NOBODY IN THEIR RIGHT MIND WOULD WANT TO SIMULATE US!
MY SPEECH WAS WITTY, SHARP AND TO THE POINT. IT FELL ON DEAF EARS—
WELL, WELL, WELL— QUITE THE LITTLE TALKER, ISN'T HE? QUITE-THE-LITTLE-TALKER.
A VERY DOUBTFUL CHARACTER. VERY DOUBTFUL INDEED.
WHAT WAS HE TALKING ABOUT, ANYWAY? WHO IS HE?
WANNA FIGHT?
ULP!
SARCASTIC PARTY
DOUBTFUL PARTY
STUPID PARTY
TALK, TALK, TALK! WE IN THE ANGRY PARTY ARE SICK AND TIRED OF TALK! IT'S TIME WE HAD SOME ACTION, SEE—ACTION!
YOU WANT ACTION—WE'LL GIVE YOU ACTION!
ANGRY P
FUN
FUN·PARTY
X·MAS·PARTY

FORGET THAT STUFFY OLD DEBATE! THE BOYS IN THE FUN PARTY HAVE BROUGHT ALONG THEIR INSTRUMENTS— AND THEY'RE RARING TO GO! SO STRAIGHT OFF LET'S GO LATIN WITH—
THE COPACOBANA SAMBA!
BOOM-BA BOOM-BA BOOM-BA
EVERYBODY DANCE! SWAY TO THAT RHYTHM! WIGGLE WITH THAT BEAT!
MR SPEAKER, I PROTEST! CAN'T WE HAVE A SLOWER NUMBER?
BOOM-PA BA! BOOM-PA BA!
BOOM-PA BA
BOOM PAH! BOOM PAH!
BOOM-BOOM-BOOM-PAH!
WE'LL GET NO SENSE OUT OF THEM NOW, DASH IT! AS FAR AS I'M CONCERNED THE WAR IS ON!
GENE
GENERAL
JUST AS SOON AS YOU'RE READY, OLD BOY! WE'LL SHOW YOUR CHAPS A THING OR TWO!
AND THAT, PUZZLED READERS, WAS THAT. WITHOUT BIG BRAIN IN CONTROL, THE WHOLE OF VERDUS WAS GOING HAYWIRE...
WHY DIDN'T I JUST CHECK MYSELF INTO A MADHOUSE AND BE DONE WITH IT?
WHY DID I HAVE TO COME TO THIS CRAZY PLANET?
WHY, WHY, WHY?
IT WAS CUTIE, MY ROBOMETER, WHO SUMMED IT UP BEST—
GEE, SAM, IT MAKES YOU KIND OF ASHAMED TO BE A ROBOT.
NEXT PROG: THIS IS WAR!

SAM SLADE HERE AGAIN, WITH A SHAVE AND A FRESH CIGAR. AND BELIEVE ME, THAT'S A LUXURY ON THE PLANET VERDUS— WHERE THE ROBOTS ARE GOING TO WAR TO DECIDE IF HUMANS REALLY ARE HUMAN! IF THAT SOUNDS CRAZY, YOU WANT TO SPEND A FEW WEEKS ON VERDUS AND THEN SEE HOW IT GRABS YA. LET ME SET THE SCENE...
ROBO HUNTER
IN THE BLACK CORNER, THE MIGHTY SECOND ARMY— ANTI-HUME! THEY THINK WE'RE ONLY IMITATION HUMANS—AND THEY LOOK LIKE THEY'VE GOT THE MUSCLE TO PROVE IT...
WE ARE THE MIGHTY SECOND, FIGHTERS THROUGH AND THROUGH! WE'RE TOUGH AND MEAN, WE DON'T FIGHT CLEAN— WE'LL ROLL ALL OVER YOU!
2000 A.D. Credit Card:
SCRIPT ROBOT T.B. GROVER
ART ROBOT I. GIBSON
LETTERING ROBOT STEVE POTTER
COMPU-73E
WE'RE THE FIGHTING FIRST AND WE NEVER GIVE AN INCH! WE'RE THE DROIDS TO CALL ON IF YOU'RE EVER IN A PINCH! UP, DROIDS, AND AT 'EM! AT 'EM, DROIDS, AT 'EM!
IN THE WHITE CORNER, THE FIGHTING FIRST ARMY— LOYAL TO A DROID AND HOT TO TROT...

FIRST BLOOD—OR SHOULD I SAY FIRST OIL— WENT TO THE WHITES...
FIRE!
RETURN FIRE!
KZZZZT!
KRRRZZZ
THEY GOT PAID BACK IN SPADES AND THE BATTLE WAS ON!
I'LL SAY ONE THING FOR THOSE VERDUS ROBOTS — THEY KNEW THE MEANING OF...
TOTAL WAR!
FIRE TWO!
ZZZT!
ALL THAT ROBOT DESTRUCTION SHOULD HAVE BEEN MUSIC TO THE EARS OF AN OLD ROBO-HUNTER LIKE ME. IT WAS... EXCEPT FOR ONE THING—

I HAPPENED TO BE RIGHT IN THE MIDDLE OF IT!
DASHED GOOD IDEA TO BRING YOU ON THIS INSPECTION TOUR, MR SLADE, SIR. DO THE TROOPS GOOD TO SEE THE HUMANS THEY'RE FIGHTING FOR.
WHAT'S THE SITUATION, COLONEL?
BAD, SIR! WE'VE TAKEN HEAVY LOSSES!
I'VE HAD TO SEND FOR A UNIT OF COMMANDOS TO STOP A BREAK-THROUGH ON THIS FLANK.
COLONEL
HUP, TWO, THREE, FOUR! WE LIKE FIGHTING, WE LIKE WAR! HUP, TWO, THREE, FOUR!
THE COMMANDOS, BY JOVE! THE FINEST FIGHTING UNIT KNOWN TO MAN OR DROID! THEY'LL SOON SORT OUT THOSE SECOND ARMY WALLAHS!
YOU THERE — YOU'RE NOT DAMAGED! WHY AREN'T YOU FIGHTING?
I'M A CONSCIENTIOUS OBJECTOR, SIR!
WE'VE HAD A LOT LIKE THIS, GENERAL. CIRCUIT BLOW-OUT, I'M AFRAID.
MEDIC
ATTENTION ALL UNITS! SEVERAL CASES OF COWARDICE HAVE BEEN REPORTED TO ME! I FORBID IT, D'YOU HEAR!
BALLY CONCHIE, BY GAD! COWARDICE, I CALL IT! WELL, I WON'T HAVE IT IN MY ARMY, YOU HEAR? I ORDER YOU TO SELF-DESTRUCT!
YES, SIR...
ZZZZZZT!
TAKE AN EXAMPLE FROM YOUR GENERAL — DO I QUAIL IN THE FACE OF THE ENEMY? DO I EVER RUN FROM A SCRAP? NEVER! I DO NOT EVEN KNOW THE MEANING OF FEAR, BY GAD!

GENERAL— THE COMMANDOS HAVE BEEN **CRUSHED!** SECOND ARMY WAR WAGONS —COMING THIS WAY...
WHAT? WAR WAGONS, YOU SAY? COMING **THIS** WAY?

NATURALLY, I'D LIKE TO STAY AND HELP YOU, MEN, BUT I'VE, ER ... JUST BEEN **CALLED AWAY.** GOOD LUCK. FIGHT TO THE LAST DROID!
DRIVE, CORPORAL! DRIVE!

HERE THEY COME!
THAT DIRTY YELLOW ROBO-RAT'S RUN OFF AND LEFT US!
YOU BETTER SCRAM, TOO, KIDD. THINGS ARE GONNA GET **ROUGH** AROUND HERE. A LITTLE GUY LIKE YOU COULD GET **HURT—**

ON SECOND THOUGHTS, WHY DON'T YOU STICK AROUND?

ZZZZZT!
GEE, SAM, THAT WASN'T VERY NICE. WHAT IF DEAR LITTLE COMMANDER KIDD GETS **KILLED?**
IT'LL BE A FAVOUR TO HUMANITY, CUTIE.
KIDD WAS A NASTY PIECE OF WORK WHEN HE WAS MY PILOT. NOW HE WAS A ONE-YEAR-OLD, I LIKED HIM EVEN **LESS!**

BESIDES, CUTIE— KIDD'S KIND OF **VICIOUSNESS** IS EXACTLY WHAT WE NEED JUST NOW!
BLAST 'EM! BLOW THEIR CIRCUITS OUT! GIVE 'EM THE OLD ONE-THREE!

YES, THE ROBOTS DIED LIKE FLIES THAT DAY. AN' IF I DO SAY SO MYSELF, YOUR OLD PAL SAM IS NO MEAN SWATTER—
OUR BLASTERS ARE NO USE AGAINST THAT WAR WAGON! GIVE ME COVERING FIRE!
EXCUSE ME, BUT—
ZZZZZT!
THE ROBOTS ARE EXPECTING OTHER ROBOTS. IT'LL TAKE THEM A WHILE TO ADJUST THEIR SIGHTS TO ME —I HOPE!
MADE IT INSIDE—NOW TO WAIT FOR THEM TO PASS...
HEY, BUDDY— CATCH!
STRAIGHT DOWN THE HATCH—
F-WHOOMP!
NICE WORK, SLADE. YOU MOVE FAST FOR AN OLD MAN!
I JUST WANTED TO SHOW THE ROBOTS THAT WAR WAGONS AREN'T SO HARD TO BEAT.
YOU'RE WRONG. AS I WAS GOING TO SAY BEFORE YOU RAN OFF, THAT IS NOT A WAR WAGON—
THAT BUILDING'S FALLING— LOOK OUT!
HEY, THE GROUND'S SHAKING! WH-WHAT'S HAPPENING?

THAT IS A WAR WAGON!
HOLY JOE SMITH! GET ME OUTTA HERE!
ER... ALL RIGHT IF I GO HOME NOW?
NEXT PROG: HOT-SHOT FOR CUTIE!

ROBO HUNTER
SAM SLADE'S THE NAME—AT LEAST I THINK IT IS! BUT ON VERDUS, THE ROBOT PLANET, SOMETIMES EVEN THE SIMPLEST THINGS ARE HARD TO REMEMBER...
MASTER SAM, WAKE UP.
WAKEY WAKEY, SLADE!
OUTTA THE WAY. I'LL SNAP THE BIG LUNK OUT OF IT—
WH-WHAZZIT? WHERE AM I?
WHERE D'YA THINK, STUPID? YOU'RE A PRISONER OF THE SECOND ROBOT ARMY!
IT ALL CAME BACK TO ME WITH THE FORCE OF A LEFT HOOK TO THE JAW. WE'D BEEN FIGHTING ALONGSIDE THE LOYAL TROOPS OF THE FIRST ROBOT ARMY, WHEN—
HOLY JOE SMITH—A WAR WAGON! LET'S GET OUTTA HERE!
BUT THERE WAS NO ESCAPE!
AT LEAST WE'LL TAKE SOME OF THEM WITH US. HIT 'EM!
2000 A.D. Credit Card:
SCRIPT ROBOT T.B. GROVER
ART ROBOT I. GIBSON
LETTERING ROBOT S. POTTER
COMPU-73E
UGGH!
LEMME GO, YOU STINKIN' ROBO-APE!

SO THERE WE WERE IN THE ROBO-SLAMMER. I WON'T SAY OUR PROSPECTS WERE BLEAK, BUT I DIDN'T NOTICE ANYONE TRYING TO SELL US LIFE INSURANCE!
YOU'VE MESSED THINGS UP GOOD AND PROPER THIS TIME, DUM-DUM. SAM SLADE, ROUGH, TOUGH ROBO-HUNTER — THAT'S A LAUGH AN' A HALF!
YOU SHOULDN'T TALK TO SAM LIKE THAT, KIDD. IT'S NOT HIS FAULT.
YOU TELL HIM, CUTIE... AN' I'LL BOP HIM!
BUT BEFORE I COULD GIVE THE LITTLE TYKE A MATCHING SET OF BOXED EARS—
GENERAL 2 WANTS YOU. COME— IMMEDIATELY.
COLONEL
GENERAL 2 WAS LEADER OF THE SECOND ARMY. HE THOUGHT THAT HUMANS WERE ONLY SIMS — SIMULATED HUMANS—AND HAD SWORN TO WIPE US OUT!
YOU DASHED SIMS HAVE CAUSED ME A LOT OF TROUBLE. YOUR LIQUIDATION WILL TAKE PLACE IN ONE HOUR.
GENE
2
KILL
TAP! TAP!
COULDN'T YOU MAKE IT TWO HOURS — I'VE GOT AN APPOINTMENT WITH MY HAIRDRESSER!
CUTIE, MY ROBOMETER, PLEADED FOR THE DEFENCE. SHE'D HAVE WRUNG TEARS FROM A STONE...
PLEASE, GENERAL, I BEG YOU TO RECONSIDER. I'VE KNOWN SAM ALL MY LIFE AND I SWEAR HE'S HUMAN. I KNOW HE HAS HIS FAULTS, BUT ONCE YOU'VE GOT TO KNOW HIM YOU'LL LOVE HIM AS MUCH AS I DO.
UNFORTUNATELY, GENERAL 2 WAS NO STONE!
STUFF AND NONSENSE! WON'T HEAR A WORD OF IT! MIGHT IS RIGHT IN THIS DROID'S ARMY, AND WE'RE GIVING GENERAL 1'S LOT A HAMMERING!
YES, BY THUNDER! IN FACT, I'M JUST ABOUT TO ACCEPT GENERAL 1'S SURRENDER!
GENE
CLICK!

ADMIT IT, YOU BOUNDER— YOUR FIRST ARMY IS BEATEN!
DASHED IMPERTINENCE! I WOULD DESCRIBE THE SITUATION AS... FLUID!
YOU'RE UP THE CREEK, YOU MEAN!
YOU CAD! WE'VE TAKEN A FEW SETBACKS, BUT WE WILL NEVER GIVE IN! MY TROOPS ARE LOYAL TO A DROID AND AS FEARLESS AS THEIR GREAT LEADER!
GENERAL 2 ★ KILL
GENERAL— 'B' DIVISION HAS GONE OVER TO THE ENEMY! NOW ONLY YOU CAN STOP A BREAKTHROUGH BY THE SECOND ARMY!
WHAT? ME? Y-YES, OF COURSE, I'LL BE— OWW!
GENERAL— WHAT'S WRONG?
DASHED LEG HINGE IS GIVING ME GIP! WAR WOUND YOU KNOW. I'D LIKE TO HELP, COLONEL— BUT THAT'S OUT OF THE QUESTION NOW, I'M AFRAID...
CORPORAL, GET MY STAFF TOGETHER! WE'RE MOVING HQ!
WHERE TO, GENERAL?
HOW DO I KNOW, YOU BALLY IDIOT? ANYWHERE! AS FAR AWAY AS POSSIBLE!
HE'S RUNNING SCARED, THE BALLY COWARD! BUT WE'LL GET HIM, BY JOVE!
TAKE THE PRISONERS AWAY UNTIL THE LIQUIDATION VATS ARE READY!

WE WAITED IN THAT BARE CELL AS THE MINUTES TICKED BY. THINGS LOOKED BLACK...
WAAAH!
THERE THERE, YOUNG MASTER, DON'T CRY. OH, THOSE WICKED WICKED ROBOTS! OH, I COULD JUST SMACK THEM!
IT'S THE WAITING I HATE. IF ONLY I HAD A WEAPON—SOMETHING TO FIGHT THEM WITH...
BUT, SAM... YOU DO HAVE A WEAPON—YOU HAVE ME.
YOU, CUTIE? I DON'T UNDERSTAND—
DON'T YOU REMEMBER, SAM? ALL QT4 ROBOMETERS HAVE AN EXPLOSIVE DEVICE BUILT-IN INSIDE. IT'S MEANT FOR EMERGENCIES JUST LIKE THIS.
NO, CUTIE— I... I COULDN'T. NOT YOU... NOT AFTER ALL WE'VE BEEN THROUGH TOGETHER.
PLEASE, SAM, YOU MUST. I'D NEVER FORGIVE MYSELF IF I LET YOU DIE.
SUDDENLY—
2
COLONEL
THE LIQUIDATION VATS ARE READY. COME.

GOODBYE...
WHOOMF!
CUTIE!

SHE WAS GONE. GONE FOREVER. THE ONLY REAL FRIEND I EVER HAD—

DAMN YOU, ROBOTS! DAMN YOU!

COME ON! LET'S MAKE IT ALL WORTHWHILE!

NEXT PROG: SLADE GOES KILL-CRAZY

I'M A PEACEABLE SORT OF GUY. TREAT ME RIGHT AND I'M AS DOCILE AS A PET SPANIEL. BUT THE ROBOTS ON VERDUS DON'T UNDERSTAND THAT . . .
NO, THE ROBOTS ON VERDUS – THEY MAKE ME MAD . . .
COME AND GET IT, YOU MURDERING ROBO-SCUM !

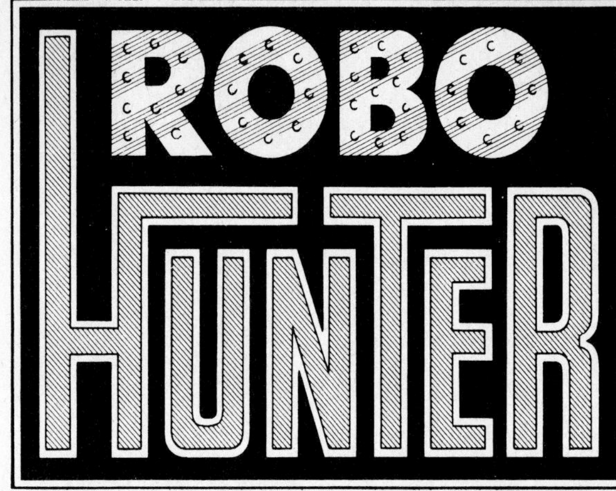

ROBO HUNTER

CUTIE WAS MY ROBOMETER, THE ONLY REAL **FRIEND** I EVER HAD. NOW SHE WAS DEAD – AND THE **SECOND ARMY** ROBO-RATS WERE GONNA PAY !

SLADE'S THE NAME – THAT'S S-L-A-Y-E-D TO YOU !

ZZZZZZZT !

AN OLD JOKE, I KNOW – BUT IT GETS BETTER EVERY TIME I TELL IT.

2000 A.D.
Credit Card:
SCRIPT ROBOT *T B GROVER*
ART ROBOT *I GIBSON*
LETTERING ROBOT *THOM*
COMPU·73E

CUTIE HAD SACRIFICED HERSELF TO GET ME OUT OF ROBO-JAIL ... AND NO WAY WOULD THOSE HUME-HATING DROIDS GET ME BACK THERE !
THE PRISONERS ARE LOOSE !
MORE OF YOU, EH ?

KRZZZZTTT !
WELL, THERE'S PLENTY HERE TO GO ROUND !
ZZZZRITT !

THE ROBOTS KEPT COMING AND I KEPT BLASTING. I GUESS I'D GONE KINDA KILL-CRAZY!
ZZZTTT!
KKKFFFTT!
KIDD, OF COURSE, LOVED EVERY MINUTE OF IT – VICIOUS LITTLE BRUTE!
ATTABOY, SLADEY! GIVE IT TO 'EM! YEHAAA! GO GO GO!
COME ON, GET UP AND FIGHT, YOU ROBO-COWARDS! GET UP, I TELL YA!
THEY CAN'T, MASTER SAM. THEY'RE DEAD. OH YES, VERY DEAD INDEEDLY!
WELL, THERE'S BOUND TO BE OTHERS ABOUT. I'LL TAKE 'EM ALL – THE MORE THE MERRIER!
OH NO, MASTER SAM. OH, MY CIRCUITS – NO! YOU MUST GET OUT OF HERE WHILE THERE'S STILL TIME.
SMOKIN' JOE'S RIGHT. EVEN YOU CAN'T HOLD OUT FOREVER. C'MON, STOP ACTING LIKE A STUPID HUMAN AND LET'S MOVE SHOE.
OH, ALL RIGHT. BUT GEE, WHOSE SIDE ARE YOU GUYS ON?

THERE WERE TWO ROBOTS GUARDING THE EXIT. I'D HOPED FOR MORE!
THE SCENE OUTSIDE BEGAN TO BRING ME TO MY SENSES. VERDUS WAS AT WAR — THE LOYAL FIRST ARMY AGAINST THE ANTI-HUME SECOND ARMY — AND THESE ROBOTS DIDN'T DO ANYTHING BY HALVES.
WHAT A MESS! THERE ISN'T GOING TO BE A PLANET LEFT BY THE TIME THOSE STINKIN' ROBOTS ARE FINISHED!
THERE THEY ARE! DESTROY THEM!
COME ON — THIS WAY!
HURRY UP, SMOKIN' JOE!
I WASN'T BUILT FOR SPEED, MASTER SAM! SAVE YOURSELVES — GO ON WITHOUT ME...
I'M FALLING! OH, MY CIRCUITS, LOOK OUT —

OWW! YOU STUPID HEAP OF JUNK!
OH DEAR! OH, MY CIRCUITS, HELP!

EVERYBODY OKAY?
I'VE LOST MY GEAR LEVER, MASTER SAM, AND MY PAINTWORK'S SCRAPED, AND—
STOW IT! LET'S CONCENTRATE ON HOW WE GET OUTTA HERE...

THAT'S EASY- TAXI!
FOR A PAIR OF ROBOT BOOTS, HE WAS SURE FOND OF TAXIS. ON EARTH HE'D HAVE NEEDED A BIG, FAT EXPENSE ACCOUNT!
A FARE! OH BOY, THIS IS MY LUCKY DAY!
OURS TOO, PAL! GET MOVING!

SAY, HAVEN'T I PICKED YOU UP BEFORE? YEAH, THAT'S RIGHT – YOU'RE THAT ROBOT THAT LOOKS LIKE A SIM, AIN'T YOU?*
WHADDYA MEAN ROBOTS? WE'RE –UNNNG!
YOU'RE RIGHT, CAB. NICE OF YOU TO REMEMBER.
*THARG-NOTE: SEE PROG 82
NEVER FORGET A FACE. STRANGE THAT, ME PICKING YOU UP TWICE...
STILL, A LOT OF STRANGE THINGS BEEN HAPPENING LATELY. LIKE ALL THIS FIGHTING. WHAT'S IT ALL ABOUT, I ASK YOU?
DIDN'T YOU KNOW – THERE'S A WAR ON.
A WAR, EH? YOU DON'T SAY. WELL, WELL, WELL, WHAT D'YOU THINK OF THAT? WHATEVER NEXT, I ASK YOU?
I WAS ASKING MYSELF THE SAME QUESTION. SOMEHOW, I HAD TO FIGURE OUT A WAY TO STOP THE WAR AND BRING THE PLANET BACK TO SANITY –
–AND FRANKLY, FOLKS, I DIDN'T KNOW WHERE TO START...
NEXT PROG: RADIO, RADIO!

ROBO HUNTER
THE ROBOTS ON VERDUS WERE AT WAR— AND YOUR OLD PAL, SAM SLADE, HAD TO THINK OF A WAY TO RESTORE A LITTLE SANITY TO THE CRAZY PLANET. IT WASN'T GOING TO BE EASY— 'SPECIALLY WITH A TALKATIVE ROBO-CAB NATTERING AWAY IN MY EAR...
... SO I SAID TO THIS GARAGE ROBOT, I SAID TO HIM: "LISTEN, PAL, THERE'S NOTHING WRONG WITH MY SUPERCHARGE. THE ONLY THING WRONG AROUND HERE IS YOU."
"AND ANOTHER THING," I SAID, "I'M A REGULAR CUSTOMER ROUND HERE AND I DEMAND A LITTLE CIVILITY— A LITTLE COMMON COURTESY, ONE ROBOT TO ANOTHER."
KNOW WHAT I MEAN, PAL? LIKE, IT DOESN'T TAKE MUCH TO SAY "GOOD MORNING" AND "PLEASE" AND "THANK YOU". THESE YOUNG ROBOTS TODAY— I DON'T KNOW WHAT THE WORLD'S COMING TO, I'LL TELL YOU...
LISTEN, CAB, I DON'T WANT TO BE RUDE BUT I'M TRYING TO THINK. HOW ABOUT A LITTLE SILENCE, HUH?
SURE, PAL. I'LL PLAY A LITTLE MUSIC. THE FRANKIE DROID SHOW IS ON THE RADIO.
THE ONLY THING THAT WILL BRING SANITY TO THIS PLANET IS TO GET RID OF THE ROBOTS— ALL OF THEM! BUT THERE'S NO WAY TO DO THAT... UNLESS ... UNLESS...
THAT'S IT— THE RADIO.
I'VE GOT YOU UNDER MY CHROME...
I'VE GOT YOU DEEP IN MY CIRCUITRY...
CAB— TAKE US TO THE RADIO STATION!
SO DEEP IN MY PARTS, YOU'RE RIGHT AT THE HEART OF ME...
WHAT'RE YOU UP TO, SLADE? ANOTHER ONE OF YOUR SCREWBALL SCHEMES?
KEEP YOUR DIAPER ON, KIDO! YOU'LL FIND OUT WHEN WE GET THERE.
2000 A.D. Credit Card:
SCRIPT ROBOT T.B. GROVER
ART ROBOT I. GIBSON
LETTERING ROBOT S. POTTER
COMPU-73E

BUT LIKE THEY SAY, GETTING THERE IS HALF THE FUN—
THERE'S SOMEONE FLASHING US DOWN. LOOKS LIKE AN ARMY VEHICLE. BETTER PULL OVER.
DARN! I HOPED WE'D LOST THEM...
IT WAS THE SECOND ARMY, OF COURSE— THE BAD GUYS. I THOUGHT FAST—
DON'T STOP, CAB. THAT'S NO ARMY VEHICLE. THEY'RE, UH...UH... AUTOGRAPH HUNTERS.
AUTOGRAPH HUNTERS? I DON'T GET YOU, PAL.
WHEN THE CHIPS ARE DOWN I CAN TELL A PRETTY NEAT LIE—
I BETTER COME CLEAN WITH YOU, CAB. YOU SEE, WE'RE NOT WHAT WE SEEM...WE'RE ACTUALLY THE RIVETS POP GROUP IN DISGUISE.
IF THOSE AUTOGRAPH HUNTERS CATCH US THEY'LL RIP US TO BITS FOR SOUVENIRS!
THE RIVETS! GEE, WHY DIDN'T YOU SAY SO..? HANG ON!
SNAP!
THEY'RE SHOOTING! FUNNY KIND OF AUTOGRAPH HUNTERS!
YEAH, THEY GET WORSE EVERY YEAR. I'LL TRY TO PUT THEM OFF!
CONTACT ALL UNITS! INFORM THEM WE'VE FOUND THE ESCAPED SIMS.*
ZZZT
KRRRZZIT!
*SIMS—SIMULATED HUMANS.

BEFORE LONG WE HAD A WHOLE POSSE ON OUR TAIL. TAXI RIDES ON EARTH WERE NEVER LIKE THIS!
BOY, YOU GUYS MUST BE REALLY POPULAR. HOW COME I'VE NEVER HEARD OF THE RIVETS?
RADIO VE
ER... WE'RE AN UNDERGROUND GROUP!
RADIOVEROUS
WE'RE HERE! EVERYBODY OUT!
ROBO CAB
GEE, YOU GUYS SURE LEAD EXCITING LIVES. YOU EVER NEED ME AGAIN, JUST GIVE ME A RING. HERE'S MY CARD.
IN THE STUDIO, THE FRANKIE DROID SHOW WAS STILL IN PROGRESS...
THAT'S WHY THE ROBOT– THAT'S WHY THE ROBOT– THAT'S WHY THE ROBOT WAS A DROID.
ON AIR
FRANKIE DROID
CLAPCLAPCLAPCLAPCLAPCLAP!
GREAT SHOW, FRANKIE — TOO BAD IT'S BEING CANCELLED...
C-CANCELLED? WHO ARE YOU? WHAT'S GOING ON?
I'M TAKING YOU OFF THE AIR! EVERYBODY SCRAM!
ERK!

THAT SHIFTED FRANKIE. VERY **HIGHLY-STRUNG,** THESE ARTISTIC ROBOTS—
UNSCREW YOUR INSTRUMENTS, BOYS. MORRIE—WE'RE LEAVING.
DON'T GO, FRANKIE— **PLEASE!**
FRANKIE DROID

I COULDN'T **POSSIBLY** GO ON AFTER THIS. MY NERVES ARE SIMPLY **SHOT TO RIBBONS.** I DON'T KNOW IF I'LL **EVER** BE ABLE TO PERFORM AGAIN.
YOU **OAF!** YOU'VE **RUINED** THE SHOW! GET OUT— **GET OUT!**
SOUNDS TECH
GET LOST!
ZZZZZT!

I DON'T KNOW WHAT YOU'RE **PLANNING,** SLADE, BUT IT BETTER BE **GOOD.**
IT WILL BE, KIDD. TAKE THIS AND GUARD THE DOOR. I'VE GOTTA GET BUSY—

THE EQUIPMENT I NEEDED WAS ALL THERE.
SOUND-WAVE ACCELERATOR.
HYPER-AMP.

VARIABLE OSCILLATOR.

WHILE KIDD GUARDED THE DOOR, BOOTS AND SJ1 — THE TWO ROBOTS WHO WERE HELPING ME — LOOKED ON...
WHAT KIND OF DEVICE ARE YOU MAKING, SLADE?
IT'S CALLED AN AMSTRANG OSCILLATOR. IT GENERATES **HIGH-FREQUENCY** SOUND WAVES POWERFUL ENOUGH TO **BLOW OUT** ROBOT CIRCUITS.
IT'S BANNED ON EARTH BECAUSE IT DESTROYS EVERY ROBOT AND COMPUTER WITHIN RANGE — FRIEND AND ENEMY ALIKE.

WHAT — YOU MEAN ME AND SJ1, **TOO?**
'FRAID SO, BOOTS.

THANKS, SLADE. THANKS A BUNDLE. I MEAN, THAT'S REALLY FRIENDLY OF YOU.

BOY, WHY DID I EVER GET INVOLVED WITH HUMANS, SJ1?
NOW, BOOTS, MASTER SAM WOULDN'T DO IT IF HE DIDN'T **HAVE TO**. IT IS A ROBOT'S **DUTY** TO DIE FOR A HUMAN. YES, YES INDEEDLY.
WE ALL BETTER BE PREPARED TO DIE IF YOU DON'T HURRY UP...

WE'RE SURROUNDED BY THE SECOND ARMY!
NEXT PROG:
BLOW-OUT!

THERE WAS ONLY ONE WAY TO RESTORE SANITY TO THE PLANET VERDUS—THE ROBOTS HAD TO BE DESTROYED! I'D GONE TO THE RADIO STATION TO BUILD A MACHINE THAT WOULD DO JUST THAT... IF I COULD FINISH IT IN TIME—AND IF IT WORKED. TWO BIG IFS...
KRRRRZZT!
HURRY UP WITH YOUR DOOMSDAY DEVICE, SLADE—THE WHOLE OF THE SECOND ARMY'S TRYIN' TO GET IN HERE!
ROBO HUNTER
2000 A.D.
Credit Card:
SCRIPT ROBOT T.B. GROVER
ART ROBOT I. GIBSON
LETTERING ROBOT S. POTTER
COMPU·73E
THE AMSTRANG OSCILLATOR WAS BANNED ON EARTH BECAUSE ITS POWERFUL HIGH-FREQUENCY SOUND WAVES BLOW OUT ALL ROBOT CIRCUITRY. BOOTS WAS NONE TOO HAPPY ABOUT THAT...
I DON'T KNOW WHY YOU'RE HELPING HIM, SMOKIN' JOE. THAT MACHINE WILL KILL US, TOO!
IT IS EVERY ROBOT'S DUTY TO DIE FOR HUMANS, BOOTS. THAT'S WHAT'S WRONG WITH THIS PLANET—YOUNG WHIPPER-SNAPPER ROBOTS DON'T KNOW THEIR DUTY. OH, MY CIRCUITS, NO!
THERE—ALL DONE. LET'S CONNECT IT TO THE RADIO TRANSMITTER—AND PRAY THAT IT WORKS!

MASTER SAM, I'VE BEEN THINKING... IF YOUR MACHINE DESTROYS ROBOTS, THEN WON'T IT—
OH! MY HAND...
BONG!
GETTING OLD, YOU KNOW. BITS OF ME ALWAYS DROPPING OFF. SHOULD HAVE BEEN SENT FOR SCRAP AGES AGO. YES, YES, INDEEDLY!
WHAT IS IT, SMOKIN' JOE?
YES... AS I WAS SAYING, IF YOUR... UH... MACHINE... UH... OH, DEAR! OH, MY OLD MEMORY BANKS! WHAT WAS I SAYING?
SCRITCH!
SCRATCH!
MEANWHILE, KIDD WAS IN TROUBLE— BIG TROUBLE!
KILL HIM!
KILL THE OTHERS!
KILL THEM ALL!
SLADE! I CAN'T HOLD 'EM! AAAGH!
NOW LET ME SEE... IT WAS SOMETHING ABOUT— NO, THAT'S NOT IT...
SORRY, SMOKIN' JOE— I CAN'T WAIT ANY LONGER...
FULL POWER
TRANSMITTER

THE OSCILLATOR SIGNALS HIT THE ROBOTS' NEURAL BANKS WITH FRIGHTENING FORCE. NO ROBOT HAD A CHANCE—
ZZZZZ
KILL...
ZZZZZZZ!
YEEHAA! YOU'VE DONE IT, SLADE!
JERK, BABY, JERK!
THE SIGNAL PENETRATED EVERYWHERE. ON THE BATTLEFIELD, WHERE GENERAL 2 WAS RECEIVING THE SURRENDER OF THE VANQUISHED FIRST ARMY—
THIS SAYS I MUST SUBMIT TO LIQUIDATION BECAUSE I'M FAULTY! WHY, YOU ABSOLUTE CAD! I'LL KILL YOU FOR THIS!
YOU AND WHOSE ARMY? JUST TRY IT!
BOUNDER!
CAD!
ZZZZZZZZZZ!
AT LAST THE GENERALS DISCOVERED THE MEANING OF... PEACE!

THE SIGNAL PENETRATED TO THE VERDUS PARLIAMENT, WHERE RABBI 1 AND THE BISHOP OF VERDUS WERE TRYING TO BRING THE ROBOTS TO THEIR SENSES...
ROBOTS, THE FUTURE OF VERDUS IS IN YOUR HANDS. YOU MUST ACT NOW TO PREVENT MORE TERRIBLE CRIMES AGAINST OUR HUMAN MASTERS.
FOR TWO BEANS I'D PUNCH HIS NOSE! DAMN IT, FOR ONE BEAN!
WHAT HUMAN MASTERS? WHAT'S HE TALKING ABOUT?
GET OFF!
SPEAKER
YOU TRY TO REASON WITH THEM, RABBI 1.
I SHOULD WASTE MY TIME ON THOSE SCHMUCKS! A THUNDER-BOLT TO STRIKE THEM DOWN, THAT'S WHAT WE NEED.
MY LIFE! WE SHOULD BE SO LUCKY!
WHAT'S HAPPENING—
ZZZZZZZ!
ZZZZZZ!
ZZZZZZ!
ZZZZZZ!
AT LONG LAST SANITY REIGNED IN THE VERDUS PARLIAMENT!

THE SIGNAL PENETRATED DEEP INTO THE BOWELS OF THE PLANET, WHERE **B.O.**, THE SEWER ROBOT, OPERATED HIS **'GIANT SEWERGATOR.'**

FORTY YEARS WE'S BEEN ALONE DOWN HERE. IT ISN'T FAIR, IS IT, B.O.? NO, NO, WE GET SO **LONELY**, DOESN'T WE?

WE WANTS TO **GET OUT!** BUT WE'S **STUCK** HERE IN THE SEWERS ON OUR OWNSOMES. HOW DOES WE GET OUT?

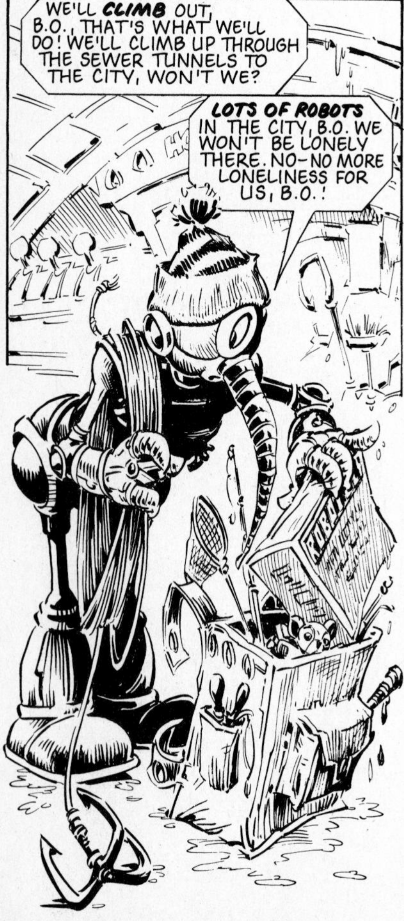

WE'LL **CLIMB** OUT, B.O., THAT'S WHAT WE'LL DO! WE'LL CLIMB UP THROUGH THE SEWER TUNNELS TO THE CITY, WON'T WE?
LOTS OF ROBOTS IN THE CITY, B.O. WE WON'T BE LONELY THERE. NO-NO MORE LONELINESS FOR US, B.O.!

WE'S SO **HIGH**, ISN'T WE, B.O.? BUT WE'S GOING TO THE CITY—WE'S GOING TO HAVE **LOTS OF FRIENDS!** SO UP WE GOES!

FOR POOR B.O., THE END WAS MERCIFULLY QUICK—
ZZZZZ! WE'S FALLING, B.O., ISN'T WE? WE'S—
ZZZZZZZT!

BACK AT THE RADIO STATION, ALL WAS QUIET—
I GOTTA HAND IT TO YOU, SLADE— YOU MAY BE A CREEP, BUT WHEN YOU HIT 'EM, YOU REALLY KNOCK 'EM DEAD!
YEAH. PITY ABOUT BOOTS AND SMOKIN' JOE. IF IT HADN'T BEEN FOR THEM WE'D HAVE BEEN DEAD MEAT LONG AGO.

HEY, SLADE, LOOK— SMOKIN' JOE'S STILL TWITCHING. KINDA FUNNY, AIN'T IT?
TWITCHING? LEMME SEE...

YOU'RE RIGHT! HE IS... BUT HE SHOULDN'T BE— UNLESS...

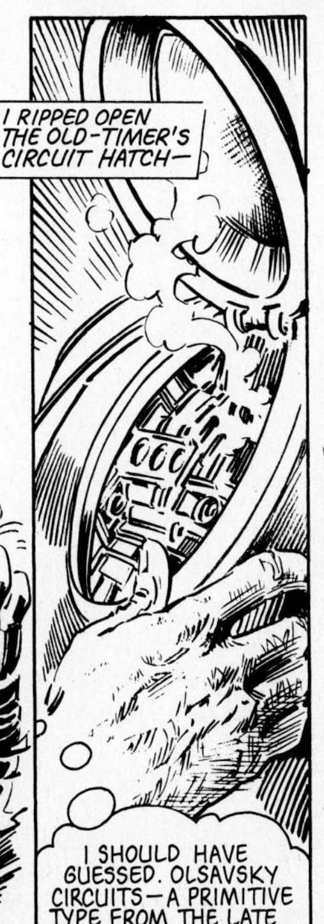

I RIPPED OPEN THE OLD-TIMER'S CIRCUIT HATCH—

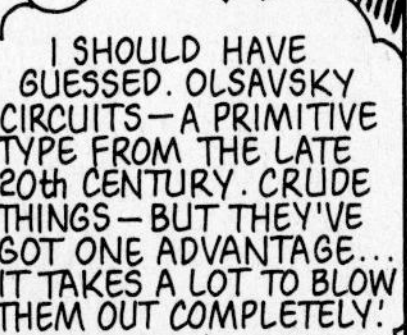

I SHOULD HAVE GUESSED. OLSAVSKY CIRCUITS— A PRIMITIVE TYPE FROM THE LATE 20th CENTURY. CRUDE THINGS— BUT THEY'VE GOT ONE ADVANTAGE... IT TAKES A LOT TO BLOW THEM OUT COMPLETELY!

GET ME MY TOOLS, KIDD. IF I WORK FAST THERE'S STILL A CHANCE I CAN SAVE HIM!

NEXT PROG:
KIDD'S REVENGE!

ROBO HUNTER
THE ROBOTS ON THE PLANET VERDUS WERE DEAD, THANKS TO A TYPICAL TOUCH OF GENIUS FROM YOUR MODEST OLD PAL SAM SLADE, ROBO-HUNTER EXTRAORDINAIRE. ALL EXCEPT ONE, THAT IS— ROBOT SJI. I WAS KINDA FOND OF OLD SMOKIN' JOE. I WORKED HARD TO SAVE HIM...
STATIC ROD, KIDD... C'MON, SNAP IT UP!
2000 A.D. Credit Card:
SCRIPT ROBOT T.B. GROVER
ART ROBOT IAN GIBSON
LETTERING ROBOT STEVE POTTER
COMPU-73E
OKAY, OKAY. KEEP YOUR WIG ON, SLADE!
I'LL HAVE TO BYPASS A LOT OF THESE BURNT-OUT CIRCUITS. IT MEANS SMOKIN' JOE WILL ALWAYS BE A BIT... GAGA. YOU KNOW — CRAZY!
SO WHAT'S NEW?
LOOK— THE OLD JUNK-HEAP'S TRYIN' TO SAY SOMETHING—
HUU... HUUUM... HUMM...
ZZZZZIT!

HUMPTY DUMPTY IDDLY UMPTY I DA LI DE O. BIG WHITE HORSE. BIG WHITE HORSE.

WHEN I WAS YOUNG AND IN MY PRIME, I KISSED THE GIRLS AND MADE THIS RHYME—

HUMPTY DUMPTY IDDLY UMPTY I DA LI DE O. MAIL BOX, POST OFFICE, BIG WHITE HORSE, **HUMPTY DUMPTY-IDDLYUMPTY-HUMPTY!**

OUTSIDE, IT WAS LIKE A SCENE OUT OF HELL. **ALL VERDUS WAS IN FLAMES—**

WHEN I DESTROYED THE ROBOTS I DESTROYED THE ROBOT FIRE BRIGADES, TOO! **NOTHING** WILL CONTROL THOSE FLAMES, NOW.

VERDUS IS BURNING—HA, HA, HA! OH, THAT'S RICH! HA, HA, HA! **HA, HA, HA, HA, HA!**

WHAT'S SO FUNNY, KIDD?

FUNNY! I'LL TELL YOU WHAT'S FUNNY—HA, HA, HA! BIG SAM SLADE, BIG, TOUGH ROBO-HUNTER—CAME TO **SAVE** VERDUS FOR THE GOOD OF HUMANITY... **HA, HA, HA!**

LOOK AT IT—HA, HA, HA! **THERE AIN'T GONNA BE NOTHING LEFT TO SAVE! HA, HA, HA, HA, HA!**

SWEET GUY, THAT KIDD. BUT I HAD TO ADMIT THAT I SAW THE FUNNY SIDE OF THINGS—UNTIL I REMEMBERED THE OTHER HUMANS ON THE PLANET...

BOY, YOU'RE GONNA BE **REAL POPULAR** WHEN WE GET BACK TO **EARTH,** SLADE! HA, HA, HA!

SAVE IT, KIDD. THOSE PEOPLE THE ROBOTS CAGED UP IN THE EXPERIMENTATION COMPLEX—**THEY'RE RIGHT IN THE MIDDLE OF THE FIRE!**

BY THE TIME WE GOT THERE, IT WAS TOO LATE—

NO-ONE'S COMING OUT OF THERE ALIVE!

POOR DEVILS. BUT MAYBE IT'S FOR THE BEST—THE ROBOTS HAD TURNED THOSE PEOPLE INTO SOMETHING LESS THAN HUMAN.

WE HEADED FOR THE SPACE DROME—
MASTER SAM, REMEMBER WHEN YOU WERE DESTROYING THE ROBOTS AND I SAID SOMETHING BAD MIGHT HAPPEN..?
YES.
WELL, I'VE REMEMBERED WHAT IT WAS... IF YOU DESTROY ROBOT CIRCUITS, THEN WON'T YOU...

...UH... UH... WON'T YOU... OH, MY OLD MEMORY BANKS! I'VE FORGOTTEN AGAIN!
NEVER MIND, SMOKIN' JOE. I'M SURE YOU'LL REMEMBER SOMEDAY.

IT TOOK US TWO DAYS TO REACH THE SPACE DROME ON FOOT, BUT IT WAS WORTH IT. OUR SHIP WAS WAITING, JUST WHERE WE'D LEFT HER—
ISN'T THAT A BEE-YOO-TIFUL SIGHT!
I CAN ALMOST SMELL THAT GOOD OLD POLLUTION ALREADY! EARTH, HERE WE COME!

I SHOULD HAVE KNOWN BETTER. VERDUS WASN'T FINISHED WITH US YET!
HEY, SLADE, SOMETHING'S WRONG! EVEN THE PRIMARY FUNCTIONS AREN'T WORKING.

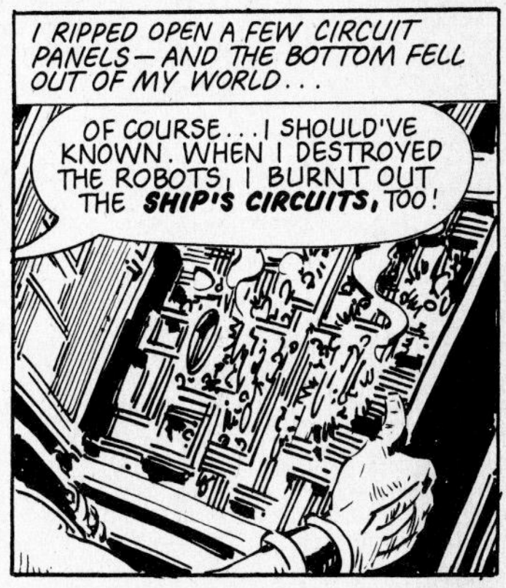
I RIPPED OPEN A FEW CIRCUIT PANELS— AND THE BOTTOM FELL OUT OF MY WORLD...
OF COURSE... I SHOULD'VE KNOWN. WHEN I DESTROYED THE ROBOTS, I BURNT OUT THE SHIP'S CIRCUITS, TOO!

MASTER SAM! I'VE REMEMBERED! I'VE REMEMBERED! IF YOU DESTROY THE ROBOTS' CIRCUITS WON'T YOU ALSO DESTROY THE CIRCUITS ON YOUR SPACE SHIP?
GOOD POINT, SMOKIN' JOE. A LITTLE LATE, BUT GOOD POINT.

NEVER MIND, MASTER SAM. HERE— HAVE SOME UMPTY CANDY.
NO THANKS, SMOKIN' JOE— I'M SLIMMING! WHY DON'T YOU JUST GO AWAY AND BANG YOUR HEAD AGAINST THE WALL OR SOMETHING?

CAN YOU FIX IT, SLADE?
MAYBE. GIVE ME A FEW DAYS AND A LOT OF LUCK, AND MAYBE— JUST MAYBE...
CLUNK-CLUNK-CLUNK!

FOR PETE'S SAKE, GO TELL THAT ROBOT TO STOP BANGING ITS HEAD AGAINST THE WALL!

WELL, FOLKS, I WON'T KEEP YOU ON THE EDGE OF YOUR SEATS. SUFFICE TO SAY THAT ONE WEEK, TWO ULCERS AND ABOUT FIVE HUNDRED CIGARS LATER, THINGS WERE LOOKING A LITTLE BETTER...
WELL, KIDD, THERE'S NOTHING FANCY ABOUT HER—BUT IF YOU'RE AS GOOD A PILOT AS YOU SAY, WE MIGHT JUST GET BACK.
I'M GOOD ENOUGH, SLADE. BUT I'M **NOT GOING!**
AT LEAST, NOT TILL I'VE HAD A LITTLE **SATISFACTION...**

YOU'VE BEEN **PUSHING ME AROUND** EVER SINCE WE GOT TO THIS PLANET. NOW I'M GONNA GET MY OWN BACK! DIG ME, LUNKHEAD?
I READ YOU, PUNK—BUT THE ANSWER'S **NO!**

IT'S YOUR CHOICE, CREEP. A **LITTLE PAIN NOW**—OR THE **REST OF YOUR LIFE** ON VERDUS!
TAKE YOUR TIME. I CAN WAIT.

NORMALLY, WHEN SOMEONE MAKES A PROPOSITION LIKE THAT YOU FIGURE THEY'RE JOKING. BUT NOT KIDD. HE **NEVER** JOKES ABOUT THINGS LIKE THAT...
ATTABOY, SLADE. A LITTLE MORE ELEVATION THERE... RIGHT—GOOD! **HOLD IT LIKE THAT!**

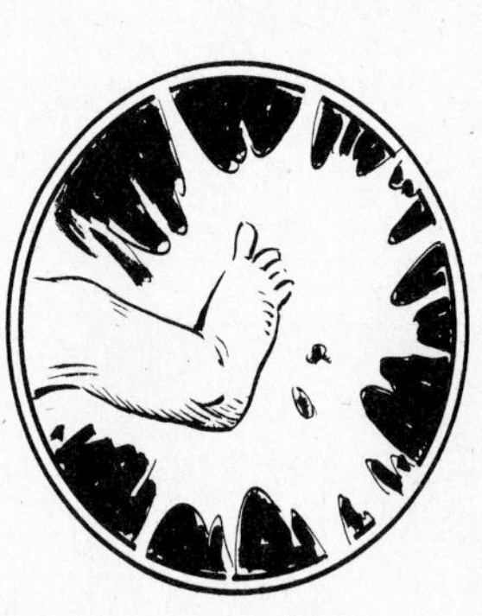

AND THERE'LL BE **MORE** WHERE THAT CAME FROM! BUT RIGHT NOW, LET'S GET THIS SHOW ON THE ROAD.

I WILL HAND IT TO KIDD—HE LIFTED THAT SHIP OFF AS NEAT AS A CAT'S TAIL. WE WERE GOING HOME AT LAST, AND NOTHING, BUT NOTHING, WAS GOING TO STOP US...
...I HOPED!
NEXT PROG: THE HEROES RETURN!

2000 A.D. Credit Card:
SCRIPT ROBOT T.B. GROVER
ART ROBOT IAN GIBSON
LETTERING ROBOT STEVE POTTER
COMPU·73E
AFTER TWO MONTHS ON THAT CRAZY ROBOT PLANET, THERE WAS NO NICER SIGHT THAN DEAR OLD EARTH LOOMING ON THE SCANNERS.
KEEP RIGHT
SURE, IT WAS POLLUTED. SURE, THERE WERE TOO MANY PEOPLE. SURE, TAXES WERE TOO HIGH AND THE WAGES TOO LOW. BUT IT WAS HOME, FOLKS—AND BELIEVE ME, HOME IS WHERE THE HEART IS...
ROBO HUNTER
MIND YOU, I WASN'T HOME YET—AS KIDD KEPT REMINDING ME...
HOW MUCH LONGER DO YOU THINK YOU CAN KEEP THIS UP, KIDD?
JUST AS LONG AS YOU NEED A PILOT TO LAND THIS SHIP, SLADE. SO STOP NARKING—I'M JUST GETTING YOU BACK FOR ALL THE THINGS YOU DID TO ME!
ROGERS AND CHAN, THE CREEPS FROM THE INTERNATIONAL SPACE COMMISSION, HAD ARRANGED A TIME-SHIELD BREAKDOWN TO RESTORE SOME OF MY LOST YOUTH. UNFORTUNATELY, COMMANDER JIM KIDD STARTED YOUNGER THAN ME. THE REVERSE AGEING TURNED HIM INTO WHAT HE WAS NOW...
...A LITTLE MONSTER!
YEEHAH! RIDE 'EM, SLADEY!
OW!
THWAK!

BUT ALL BAD THINGS MUST COME TO AN END. AT 9 IN THE MORNING WE TOUCHED DOWN AT THE JAMES CALLAGHAN MEMORIAL SPACE DROME...
WELCOME BACK, SLADE. AND ROBOT SJI, TOO! I-I SUPPOSE POOR COMMANDER KIDD IS... DECEASED?
NO SUCH LUCK, PAL. HE'S INSIDE. HE'S JUST A BIT TIED UP.
HAVE SOME UMPTY CANDY.
DANGER
KEEP CLEAR
UNDER REPAIR
SLADE
WELCOME HOME!
HOW WAS PARADISE?
NICE ONE SAM!
MMNNG! MMNNGM!
THE PRESS WERE WAITING FOR US AT SPACE COMMISSION HQ—
THAT'S ENOUGH QUESTIONS FOR NOW, GENTLEMEN.
I'VE GOT ONE QUESTION FOR YOU GUYS—
UMPTY CANDY?
WHERE ARE ALL THE FEMALE REPORTERS? I MEAN, WHEN A GUY GETS BACK TO EARTH HE EXPECTS TO SEE SOMETHING BETTER'N YOUR UGLY KISSERS!
I MIGHT HAVE KNOWN—
OH, ISN'T HE SWEET!
WHAT A LITTLE DARLING!
LET ME HOLD HIM NEXT, THELMA.
HEY! HEY, GIRLS! FORGET THAT HORRIBLE LITTLE RUNT—THERE'S A BIG STRONG HE-MAN HERE IN NEED OF A LITTLE OF YOUR CHARMS.
SQUEEZE ME TIGHTER, BABE. I WON'T BREAK!
SLAP!
SLAP!
HOW DARE YOU SPEAK LIKE THAT ABOUT HIM!
YOU BRUTE! POOR LITTLE KIDD'S TOLD US ALL ABOUT YOU!

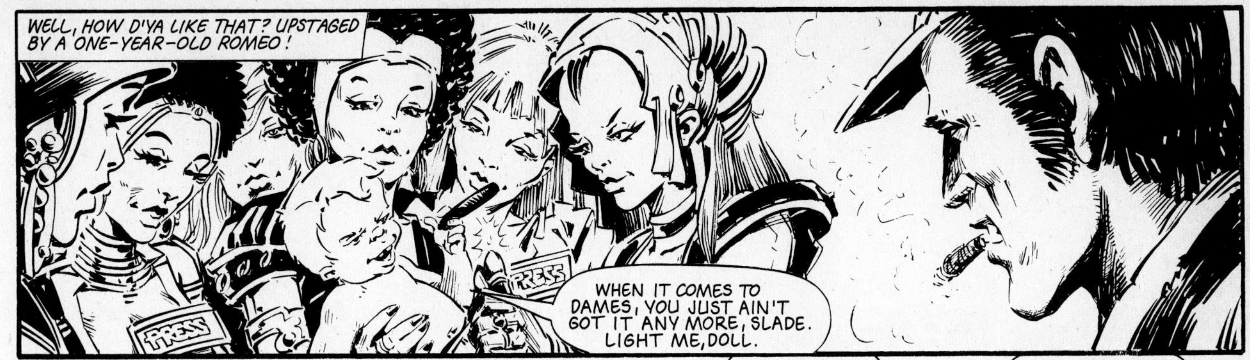
WELL, HOW D'YA LIKE THAT? UPSTAGED BY A ONE-YEAR-OLD ROMEO!
PRESS
PRESS
WHEN IT COMES TO DAMES, YOU JUST AIN'T GOT IT ANY MORE, SLADE. LIGHT ME, DOLL.

KIDD'S MOMENT OF GLORY WAS SHORT-LIVED...
ALL RIGHT, WHERE IS HE? AH, I SEE YOU- TIME FOR YOUR NAP, YOUNG MAN!
WHADDYA MEAN NAP? WH-WHAT IS THIS..?
PRESS

THE SPACE COMMISSION HAVE ASSIGNED ME TO LOOK AFTER YOU. WE'LL START BY GETTING RID OF THIS NASTY CIGAR!
BUT I DON'T NEED A STINKIN' ROBO-NANNY! I'M THIRTY-SEVEN YEARS OLD, DAMN IT!
NANDROID

THEN YOU'RE OLD ENOUGH TO MIND YOUR LANGUAGE! I'M GOING TO WASH YOUR MOUTH OUT WITH SOAP AND THEN PUT YOU STRAIGHT TO BED!
HELP!
UMPTY CANDY? TRY IT. YOU'LL LIKE IT.

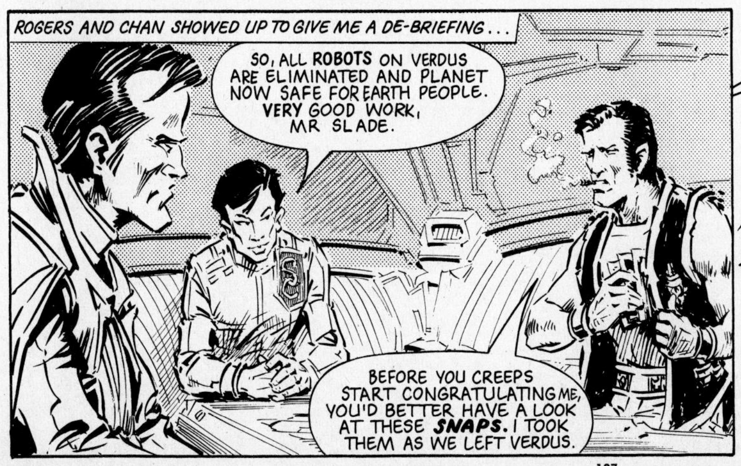
ROGERS AND CHAN SHOWED UP TO GIVE ME A DE-BRIEFING...
SO, ALL ROBOTS ON VERDUS ARE ELIMINATED AND PLANET NOW SAFE FOR EARTH PEOPLE. VERY GOOD WORK, MR SLADE.
BEFORE YOU CREEPS START CONGRATULATING ME, YOU'D BETTER HAVE A LOOK AT THESE SNAPS. I TOOK THEM AS WE LEFT VERDUS.

VERDUS HAD A SLIGHT ACCIDENT...
IT'S BURNING! THE WHOLE PLANET IS BURNING!

ALL THE WORK THE ROBOTS DID— WASTED! I'LL HAVE YOUR HEAD FOR THIS, SLADE!
ONE MOMENT, MR ROGERS. A WORD IN HONOURABLE EAR.
WE ARE ONES WHO SEND MR SLADE TO VERDUS. IT LOOK VERY BAD ON RECORDS IF MISSION GOES DOWN AS FAILURE.
YEAH... YEAH, YOU GOT A POINT THERE, CHAN. DAMN! I GUESS THERE'S ONLY ONE THING FOR IT— WE'LL HAVE TO MAKE SLADE A GOLDARNED HERO!
AND THAT, DEAR READERS, WAS HOW I CAME TO RECEIVE THE WORLD MEDAL OF HONOUR. AND THAT IS ALSO WHERE MY STORY ENDS. OH, EXCEPT FOR ONE THING. THAT AFTERNOON THEY HELD A PUBLIC RECEPTION FOR US...
THERE MUST BE A MILLION PEOPLE OUT THERE. NOT NERVOUS, ARE YOU?
YOU GOTTA BE JOKING, BUSTER.
WELL, I'M KINDA BUSY RIGHT NOW, SWEETHEART...
UMPTY CANDY?
NOT WHILE I'M ON DUTY.
GENUINE SAMSLADE CAPS ON SALE HERE!
KIDD SPOKE FIRST—
FRIENDS, WHEN THE SPACE COMMISSION FORCED ME TO FLY THIS MISSION I WAS TALL AND HANDSOME. IN MY PRIME. THE BEST DAMNED PILOT IN THE 8th FLOTILLA! I'VE BEEN THROUGH HELL AND COME BACK. AND LOOK AT ME NOW— A 37-YEAR-OLD BABY: A FREAK!
BUT AM I BITTER? DO I BEAR ANY GRUDGES?
YOU'RE TOO DAMN RIGHT I DO!

ROGERS AND CHAN ARE TO BLAME! NOW I'M GONNA GIVE THOSE RATS WHAT'S COMIN' TO THEM!
LOOK OUT!

EASY, KIDD. DON'T WANT TO HURT ANYONE, DO YOU?
YOU BET I DO! LEMME GO, SLADE! YOU GOT AS MUCH REASON TO HATE THOSE RATS AS I DO!
WELL, FOLKS, THE MORE I THOUGHT ABOUT IT, THE MORE I SAW HIS POINT. I DID HATE THOSE RATS—
OKAY, KIDD, YOU'RE OFF THE LEASH. HAVE FUN.
THANKS, SLADE. MAYBE YOU AIN'T SUCH A CREEP AFTER ALL!

COME ON, YOU COWARDS! COME OUT AND TAKE IT LIKE MEN!
UMPTY CANDY? I MADE IT MYSELF!
YEEEOW!
HELP!

WHEN THEY FINALLY GOT KIDD CALMED DOWN, IT WAS A MIRACLE NO-ONE WAS HURT. AT LEAST, NOT BADLY!
I AIN'T FINISHED WITH YOU TWO! I'LL BE BACK! THE WORLD AIN'T BIG ENOUGH TO HIDE YOU!
WHAT A SHAMBLES! GET SLADE TO SPEAK TO THE CROWD, QUIET THEM DOWN.
WHERE IS MR SLADE?
UMPTY CANDY?
DON'T YOU HAVE ANY NUTTY FUDGE?
ANDROID

WE CAN'T FIND SLADE ANYWHERE. HE'S DISAPPEARED!

ME, I SLIPPED OUT DURING THE COMMOTION. I FIGURED IF I HUNG AROUND IT'D BE QUESTIONS AND ANSWERS FOR THE NEXT MONTH. AND AFTER VERDUS, I NEEDED A **HOLIDAY**!

IT'S SO NICE TO SEE YOU AGAIN, SAM. WHERE TO?

ANYWHERE, TOOTS. JUST DRIVE!

TAX

SAY, GIRLS, THERE'S A SPOT ON MY FOREHEAD THAT AIN'T BEEN KISSED YET. THERE, JUST ABOVE THE EYEBROW...
OH, SAM, WE'VE **DONE** THERE.
ROUTE 69
CITY
"SCENIC"
SLAYED

CAUTION ATOMIZER
KEEP YOUR CITY CLEAN
WELL—DO IT AGAIN, BABE. YOUR OLD PAL SAM SURE AIN'T GONNA FILE ANY **COMPLAINTS**!
WORLD MEDAL OF HONOUR
The End

2000 AD Prog 76: Art by **Ian Gibson**

2000 AD Prog 80: Art by **Ian Gibson**

2000 AD Prog 100: Art by **Ian Gibson**

2000 AD Prog 102: Art by **Ian Gibson**

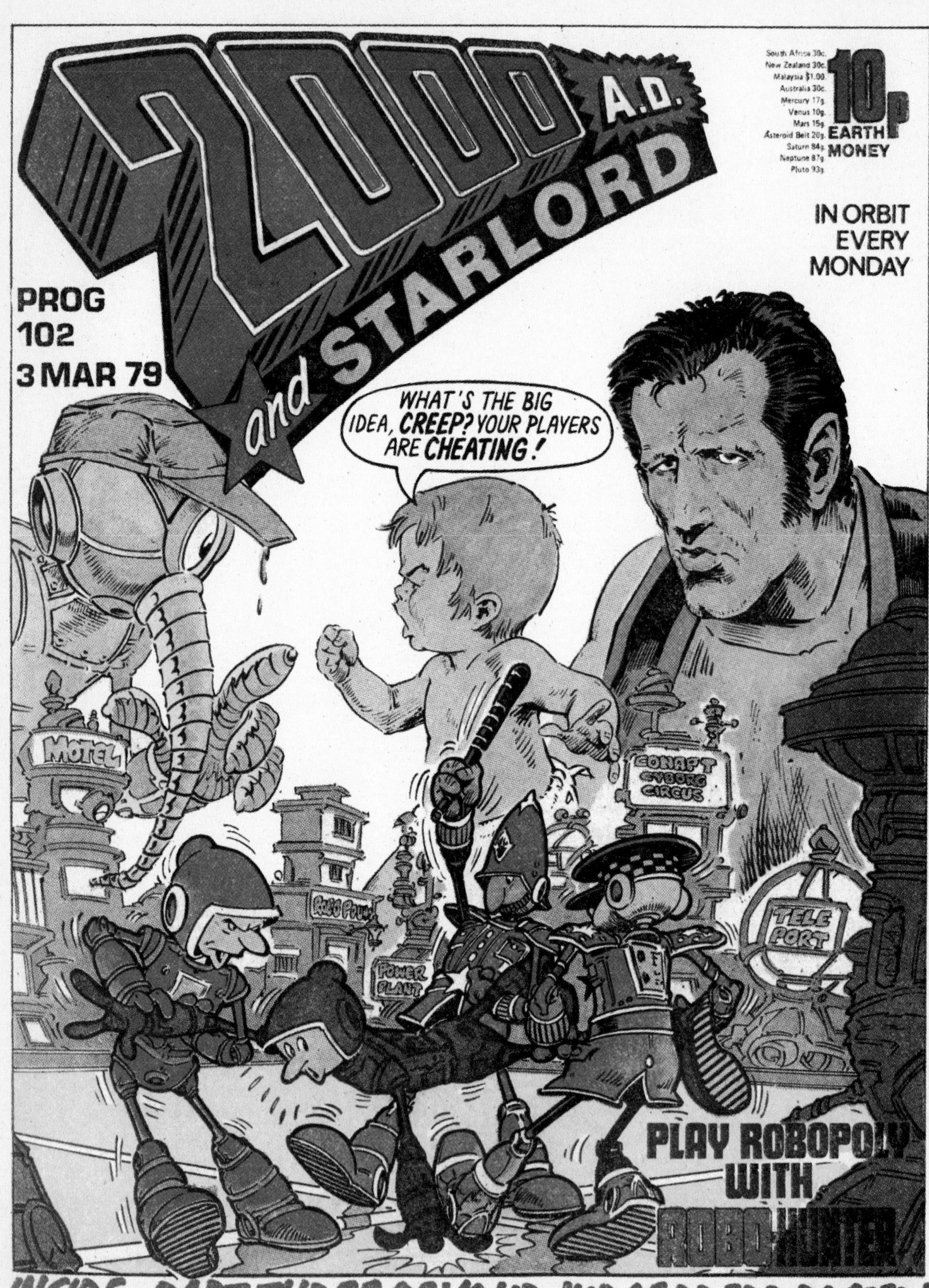

2000 AD Prog 106: Art by **Ian Gibson**

John Wagner is, to many fans, the very heart of *2000 AD*. Involved from the earliest days of the "Galaxy's Greatest Comic," he co-created *Judge Dredd* as well as *Strontium Dog*, *Robo-Hunter* and a host of other *2000 AD* mainstays, including the critically-acclaimed *Button Man*.

Incredibly prolific throughout his career, and writing under a diversity of pen names — often in concert with Alan Grant, with whom he devised and developed *2000 AD*'s sister comic, the *Judge Dredd Megazine* — Wagner has worked extensively beyond the Thargian universe, originating and editing a number of British periodicals as well as writing many American standards, including *Batman*, *The Punisher*, *Lobo* and *Star Wars* bounty hunter *Boba Fett*. A film adaptation of his Paradox Press graphic novel *A History of Violence* is scheduled to be released in 2005 from New Line Cinema.

One of *2000 AD*'s best-loved and most honored artists, **Ian Gibson** is responsible for the co-creation of *The Ballad of Halo Jones* (with Alan Moore), and created Bella Bagley, an unfortunate character in Judge Dredd's world who fell head-over-heels in love with "Old Stony Face" himself!

Of course, Gibson's involvement with *2000 AD* is far more extensive. He has worked on *Ace Trucking Co.*, *I Was a Teenage Tax Consultant*, *Judge Anderson*, *Future Shocks*, *Project Overkill*, *Robo-Hunter*, *Ro-Jaws' Robo-Tales*, *Strontium Dog*, *Maze Dumoir*, *Tharg the Mighty*, *The Mind of Wolfie Smith* and *Walter the Wobot*, as well as *The Taxidermist* in *Judge Dredd: The Megazine*. Prior to his start at *2000 AD*, Gibson illustrated Starlord's *Mind Wars* with Redondo, and he has also illustrated Judge Dredd's adventures in the *Daily Star* newspaper.

His work outside the Galaxy's Greatest Comic includes *Chronicles of Genghis Grimtoad*, *Foot Soldiers*, *Green Lantern Corps*, *Meta-4*, *Millennium* (with Joe Staton), *Mr. Miracle*, *Star Wars: Boba Fett*, *Star Wars: Droids*, *Steed and Mrs. Peel* and *X-Men Unlimited*, plus the designs for the TV series *Reboot*. He created also created Annie Droid for *The Times*.

José Luis Ferrer began his UK comics career with *Starlord*, and later co-created *Ant Wars* in *2000 AD*. He has also illustrated *Robo-Hunter* and *Tharg's Future Shocks*.